Teaching Character...

In the
Middle Grades

36 Weeks of Daily Lessons for Grades 6–8

**Sadie Allran Broome, Nancy W. Henley
Elizabeth Mordaszewski**

TEACHING CHARACTER IN THE MIDDLE GRADES: 36 Weeks of Daily Lessons for Grades 6-8

For information, contact:
Character Development Group, Inc.
P.O. Box 35136
Greensboro, NC 27425-5136
(336) 668-9373, (336) 668-9375 fax
info@charactereducation.com
www.CharacterEducation.com

Project Management by Ginny Turner
Cover design by Sara Sanders
Text editing by Ginny Turner
Page layout by Scott Turner

ISBN-10: 1-892056-18-6
ISBN-13: 978-1-892056-18-4
$24.95

Quantity Purchases
Companies, schools, professional groups, clubs and other organizations may qualify for special terms when ordering quantities of this title. For ordering information, contact the Customer Service Department of Character Development Publishing at the numbers listed above.

Dedication

To The Magic Kids, students that have touched our lives as classroom teachers. We have probably learned as much from them as they learned from us. They have been and will always be inspirational.

To Gene Dellinger, the character man in Gaston County, who promotes the tenets of character education on a daily basis. He not only talks about character and teaches character but he lives it and serves as role model for teachers and students.

> Sadie Allran Broome
> Nancy W. Henley

To my parents, Paul and Gert Fairweather, for leading me to be the "character" that I am today, with solid character traits to share with our youth. I am grateful for their guidance and continued support: I sure didn't get this way by myself!

> Elizabeth Mordaszewski

Acknowledgments

Thank you to the North Carolina Center for the Advancement of Teaching. It is a special place adjacent to the campus of Western Carolina University in Cullowhee, North Carolina. Teachers may apply to spend a week on the campus in a program called Teacher-Scholar-in-Residence Program. They provide the place, food, material, and advice to enable you to make your special project a success. The three of us would not otherwise have found the time to devote to making this book possible. This program afforded us the uninterrupted time and conditions to plan and pursue the task of writing. We will always be grateful.

Sadie Allran Broome
Nancy W. Henley
Elizabeth Mordaszewski

I would like to acknowledge my husband Dennis. He is my solid foundation from which I am able to achieve success and happiness. He is supportive and provides encouragement all along the way. —S.A.B.

I want to acknowledge the love and support I get from the other two thirds of my "home team"...Matt and Ben, I love you, guys. —N.W.H.

Thank you to my husband Richard for the fine advice and wisdom he has offered to me in recognizing character traits in people. He has given me great encouragement and has always believed in me. He has been a faithful source of care and growth during unexpected challenges. —E.M.

Table of Contents

Introduction

Teaching character traits to our middle school students is just as important as teaching the academic curriculum. Many of our students have not had an opportunity to develop a set of kind, caring, responsible behaviors for personal interaction. Middle school students, by nature, need to explore peer interactions, and they have many questions about life and relationships. Any teacher can tell you it's difficult to teach the academic curriculum effectively when you have to take time to settle classroom disruptions. The brief character lessons offered here for the middle school years are intended to develop in students over time the character traits we admire in others and would like to see in our future citizens. The more respectful behavior thus engendered would enable us to spend more quality time teaching.

We have developed these lessons over our careers, which we have spent working with students identified with behavior problems. It is our hope that they can develop in your students a core of good character that will help them in all aspects of their lives at work and at play. The activities included in this book can be used in a variety of ways. We have set up a daily structure for using the lessons in class meetings, but the ideas can also be used as additions to the daily curriculum whenever you deem appropriate. An appropriate time for these middle school lessons could be the homeroom or "connections" class. We have found it beneficial to teach students character traits in a class-meeting format each day. We used the class period to discuss a famous quote or saying, explore a character trait, and practice the concept with appropriate activities and discussion. These class meetings would help all teachers and benefit all students, not just students labeled as exceptional. Whenever possible, we encouraged students to use the character traits we were studying in other settings so they could internalize their application.

Literature citations, especially proverbs, were quite effective during the class meetings to bring the character traits to life. We found that putting the quote on the board each week gave the students several days to explore the meaning of the quote. It was always a delight when spontaneous repetitions of the quote, either the current one or earlier ones, would occur as we did our daily work. It was also a way to expose them to the great truths of our civilization and begin to point them to great literature.

As teachers, we are teaching and modeling character every day, whether we intend to or not. Our students are watching us constantly to see if we are honest and fair. Developing character is a cumulative building process. These lessons can lay a firm foundation, cement already present virtues, and make students value character as part of their daily learning.

Sadie Allran Broome

Nancy W. Henley

Elizabeth F. Mordaszewski

Helpful Hints

The following suggestions might be helpful for using these lessons in your classroom.

- The lesson plans are a guideline for a daily class-meeting format. Feel free to adapt the material to your own method of teaching—the lessons can be used in a variety of ways.

- The lessons are brief, intended to take about 10-15 minutes per day.

- We wrote the quote on the board and left it up all week. Usually, in the lesson plan format, we discussed it on Mondays. Then the students can refer to it throughout the week.

- Class activities about the different character traits can be displayed in a special place in the classroom

- For cooperative group activities, always teach a character trait along with an academic skill. Carry a checklist on a clipboard to monitor the class activities and, as you go from group to group, write notes about specific students or groups who remembered to apply the trait. Be sure to praise the ones who remembered!

The Lessons

GOAL: ## Student participates constructively in making group decisions.

"Don't just stand there, do something."

Common directive

Display the character trait for the week:
COOPERATION

Activity	Materials	Evaluation
Ask students to define the term "group decision." Record key words and phrases to use as discussion points. Lead group in developing a list of steps for making group decisions	Chart paper Markers	Student participation in discussion
Review steps from yesterday for making group decisions. Have students work in groups to follow the steps and make decisions in hypothetical situations. Let each group report and discuss.	Index cards with "decision situations" written on them	Teacher moves from group to group, noting and giving feedback on the level of cooperation.
Discuss the quote and how it applies to group decision-making. What effect does non-participation have on the process?	None	Student participation in discussion
In the classroom, the teacher makes many decisions. Record as the students name decisions that could be made by the group. After brainstorming, choose at least one item on the list you are comfortable letting the class decide.	None	Student participation in discussion
Lead the class in making a decision on an item from yesterday's list.	None	Student participation in discussion

GOAL: Student assumes responsibility for routine tasks.

"Responsibility is the price of greatness."
Winston Churchill

Display the character trait for the week:
RESPONSIBILITY

Activity	Materials	Evaluation
What is responsibility? Have students work in groups to list responsible behaviors. Share results and guide the class in developing a definition of responsibility.	Paper and markers to write and display final draft of definition	Teacher will move from group to group to observe cooperative behavior and participation.
Can we identify responsible people in our world? Have students work in groups to cut and paste pictures and articles of examples from newspapers or magazines.	Newspapers Magazines Scissors Paste Poster board	Students' "Responsibility collages"
Discuss the quote. Does the word greatness mean that one is always recognized for his/her acts? Are all responsible acts glamorous? Talk about how smaller responsibilities have great importance.	None	Student participation in discussion
Members of groups have certain responsibilities. Record as students name groups they are a part of (e.g., families, classes, clubs, neighborhoods).	Chart paper Marker	Student participation in discussion
How does one person's responsibility, or the lack of it, affect others? Have students work in groups to come up with examples. Share and discuss.	None	Participation in small-group and class discussion

GOAL: ## Student exhibits appropriate behaviors for different environments.

"Every land has its own law."

Scottish proverb

Display the character trait for the week:
GOOD JUDGMENT

Activity	Materials	Evaluation
Greet the class dressed in an atypical style for the classroom (e.g., a sports uniform). Let them whisper and giggle for a bit, then lead a discussion about appropriate dress for a given situation.	Your costume (go on...the kids will LOVE it!)	Student participation in discussion
Discuss the quote. How does this apply to yesterday's discussion? Have groups make lists of examples related to suitable dress.	Paper Pencils	Each group will have a reporter to share their findings
Refer to the quote again. Does it speak only to dress? Cite examples of cultural differences in behavior.	Examples of customs or behaviors from other cultures that differ from ours.	Student participation in discussion
Bring them back to their immediate world. Are there different "lands" within our school, that call for different types of behavior? Give examples (e.g., hall, cafeteria, library, an assembly, etc.).	None	Student participation in discussion
Have students work in groups to prepare and perform simple role plays to illustrate that a given situation calls for a certain type of behavior. Tell them you will be looking and listening for good cooperation within groups.	None	Appropriate participation in planning and perrforming the role plays

GOAL: Student follows classroom procedures.

"Don't put the cart before the horse."
Latin proverb.

Display the character trait for the week:
RESPONSIBILITY

Activity	Materials	Evaluation
Discuss the quote as an idiom. What does it mean in the literal vs. the nonliteral sense? Have students draw pictures to illustrate putting the cart before the horse.	Paper Crayons, markers or colored pencils	Student participation in discussion and student pictures
Record as students cite examples of daily routines and procedures and their sequence.	Chart paper Marker	Student participation in discussion
Why do we need prescribed procedures? What would happen in the cafeteria each day if there weren't any? Let students role-play this and other examples.	None	Participation in discussion and role plays
Choose a simple procedure in the classroom, such as getting pencils sharpened or getting assignments written down. Let groups develop their own procedures and evaluate together. If you can live with it...adopt one!	Paper Pencils	Student participation in discussion
Record as students name "problem areas" in your school. Let them work in groups to generate suggestions for procedural changes that could help. Evaluate the plans together and submit suggestions to the principal.	Paper Pencils	Student participation in discussion

GOAL: Student shows respect for authority figures.

"Courtesy costs nothing."

Ralph Waldo Emerson

Display the character trait for the week:
RESPECT

Activity	Materials	Evaluation
Have a student read aloud the definition of authority. Elicit the meaning of authority figures and record as students name examples.	Dictionary Chart paper Marker	Student participation in discussion
Why is it important to respect authority figures? Discuss each one on the list from yesterday.	Monday's list	Student participation in discussion
Is it possible to show respect to people we disagree with, or even dislike? Discuss the quote and relate it to this question through examples.	None	Student participation in discussion
Tell students you will be looking for cooperation as they work in groups to list behaviors that show respect. Share and discuss.	Paper Pencils	Teacher moves from group to group giving feedback on good cooperation and participation by all.
Have students work in groups to prepare role plays that illustrate showing respect for an authority figures in conflict or disagreement.	None	Participation in planning and performance of role plays

GOAL: ## Student assumes responsibility for his/her own actions.

"If you can't stand the heat, get out of the kitchen."
Harry S Truman

Display the character trait for the week:
RESPONSIBILITY

Activity	Materials	Evaluation
Put students in groups and give each a list of problem situations. Tell them you will be looking for good group decision-making skills as they decide who is responsible in each case. Keep these lists.	List of situations (e.g., a student borrows another's science book and forgets to return it. That night, the book owner can't do his assignment because he has no book.)	Participation in small-group discussions
Return Monday's lists to groups. Read each item and let each report their decision. Discuss, pointing out that this was at times a difficult judgment to make.	Monday's group lists	Student participation in discussion
Discuss the quote. How much more difficult is it to assign responsibility when looking at ourselves? Review some of the situations on Monday's list. Ask students to put themselves in the place of the student in each. Discuss.	Monday's group lists	Student participation in discussion
Have students work in groups to develop bumper sticker designs that encourage people to take responsibility for their own actions.	Paper Markers, crayons or colored pencils	Student products
Choose an article from the newspaper about an adult who did not take responsibility for his/her actions. Read and discuss.	Newspaper article	Student participation in discussion

GOAL: Student participates constructively in class activities.

"If you're not part of the solution, you're part of the problem."

1975, Concise Oxford Dictionary of Proverbs

Display the character trait for the week:
RESPONSIBILITY

Activity	Materials	Evaluation
Discuss the various roles that members play in a group discussion: reader, recorder, timekeeper, reporter, etc. Record as the students define the function of each.	Chart paper Marker	Student participation in discussion
Choose students to assume roles in a group and demonstrate the process for the class with a given topic. Discuss and give feedback.	Writing materials for the recorder	Participation in discussion and/or role play
Discuss the quote. Lead the discussion to relate it to the importance of participation by all.	None	Student participation in discussion
Do we have to accept roles we don't want sometimes? Is there room for us to negotiate with other group members? Have student groups prepare and do role-plays to illustrate.	None	Participation in planning and presentation of role-plays
Have student groups come up with a modified version of the quote in their own words. Share with class.	None	Participation in group discussion

GOAL: ## Student recognizes the need for fair rules and laws.

"If you want peace, work for justice."
Bumper sticker

Display the character trait for the week:
FAIRNESS

Activity	Materials	Evaluation
What do we mean when we say something is fair or unfair? List student examples.	Chart tablet with headings FAIR and UNFAIR Marker	Student participation in discussion
Announce (with a straight face) that today...all the girls will have free time during your class and the boys will do work as usual. Then stand back! When the clamor dies down, lead a discussion about fairness.	None	Student participation in discussion
Discuss the quote. Relate it to war and peace. Ask for examples of wars that have been fought over injustice. Introduce the Civil War as an example.	None	Student participation in discussion
Revisit the "event" on Tuesday. Was the "loss of peace" due to injustice? Record as students offer examples of situations between individuals in which the absence of justice created conflict.	Chart paper Marker	Student participation in discussion
Have students work in groups to make signs that complete the sentence "If you want peace..." and illustrate it. Display.	Prepared sheets with the heading "If you want peace..." Markers, crayons, or colored pencils	Student products

GOAL: Student can analyze classroom problems and come up with solutions.

"The door to success is always marked push."

Anonymous

Display the character trait for the week:
PERSEVERANCE

Activity	Materials	Evaluation
Introduce the word perseverance and discuss the quote. Give examples and record as students name situations that call for perseverance.	None	Student participation in discussion
Relate a personal story in which you solved a difficult problem by persevering. Ask students to share their own stories in small groups.	None	Student participation in discussion
Introduce and demonstrate "self-talk." Discuss how this can be a strategy to support oneself in persevering in difficult situations. Record as students give examples of positive phrases to use in "self-talk."	Chart paper Marker	Student participation in discussion
Review yesterday's list. How can affirmations be used to support others in reaching goals? Have students practice encouraging each other.	List from Wednesday's activities	Participation in discussion and practice
Have students work in small groups to resolve a classroom problem. Tell them that you'll be looking for perseverance and encouragement. Share and discuss solutions.	None	Appropriate participation and solutions

GOAL: ## Student respects likenesses and differences in others.

"To each his own."

Anonymous

Display the character trait for the week:
RESPECT

Activity	Materials	Evaluation
What is respect? How do we show people respect? Record as students name "dos and don'ts" of respect.	Chart paper Marker	Student participation in discussion
Pass out prepared lists of ten items on which students are to circle their choices. Keep these.	Copies of a list of choices: 1. Ice cream or milk? 2. Morning or evening? 3. Reading or math?, etc.	Completed student lists
Return lists from yesterday. Announce that you will now read out the "correct" answers. Use as a catalyst to a discussion of the quote.	Student lists from Tuesday	Student participation in discussion
Introduce and relate the two concepts of prejudice and diversity. Discuss.	None	Student participation in discussion
How can we celebrate diversity in our school and community? Elicit or give a few examples of ways to learn more about people who are different from ourselves, such as: sharing personal stories, visiting a different church, etc.	None	Participation in group discussion and student products

TEACHING CHARACTER IN THE MIDDLE GRADES

GOAL: ## Student can recognize examples of community service.

"Snowflakes are one of nature's most fragile things, but just look what they can do when they stick together."

Vesta M. Kelly

Display the character trait for the week:
RESPONSIBILITY

Activity	Materials	Evaluation
What is a community? Name some communities to which we all belong. What is your role in each of these?	None	Student participation in discussion
Discuss the quote. Have you ever turned snowflakes into other things by "sticking them together"? Encourage students to describe things they make in the snow—snowballs, forts—and compare their strength to the softness of flakes.	None	Student products
How does the quote relate to our roles in a community? In what ways are you responsible to others in your community?	None	Student participation in discussion
What is community service? Can kids do it? Record as students give examples. Encourage them to share personal experiences. (Share your own, too.)	Chart paper Marker	Student participation in discussion
Our school is a community to which we belong. How can we encourage school community service? Work in groups to make posters for display in the school.	Poster board Markers, crayons, or colored pencils (Paint if you dare!)	Student products

TEACHING CHARACTER IN THE MIDDLE GRADES

GOAL: ## Student can distinguish between wants and needs.

"The more you have, the more you want."
Latin proverb

Display the character trait for the week:
SELF-DISCIPLINE

Activity	Materials	Evaluation
Discuss the quote. Can you tell about a situation when this was true about you?	None	Student participation in discussion
Have students work in groups to tape items written on index cards onto one of two small posters. Display and compare. If groups have items under different headings, discuss and reach consensus.	One each of posters headed WANTS and NEEDS for each group. Identical sets of prepared cards printed: food, water, TV, sun, video games, etc. Tape	Student products and participation in large and small group discussions
Do our needs vary from one age to another? Name things that you needed when you were younger, that you don't need now, as well as things you need now that you didn't when younger.	None	Student participation in discussion
Do people ever want things that are not good for them? Record as students give examples. Let students illustrate signs headed "You don't need this..." and at the bottom: "even if you want it."	White preprinted sheets Markers, crayons, or colored pencils	Student products
Ask each student to make a personal list of things they want and things they need. Explain that they do not have to share the list. This is just for personal reflection.	Paper and pencils	Student participation

GOAL: Student can predict the consequences of responsible and irresponsible actions.

"As you make your bed, so you must lie in it."

1590, Concise Oxford Dictionary of Proverbs

Display the character trait for the week:
RESPONSIBILITY

Activity	Materials	Evaluation
What does it mean to be *responsible*? Read sentences using the word one at a time and let students paraphrase the sentences.	Prepared list of sentences with responsible (e.g., You are responsible for your baby brother. Who is responsible for this mess?)	Student participation in discussion
What are consequences? Have students work in groups to come up with examples of actions and consequences. Share and discuss.	None	Student participation in discussion
Discuss the quote. Have students make pictures to illustrate.	Paper Markers, crayons, colored pencils	Student products
Contrast responsible and irresponsible behavior, using examples, to bring in the concept of consequences. Have student groups make lists of responsible and irresponsible behaviors.	Paper Pencils	Student products
How can one person's irresponsible behaviors affect others? Give examples. Student groups search for examples in the newspaper. Discuss.	Newspapers	Student participation and articles chosen

GOAL: # Student can explain the need to apply rules fairly.

"Those who deny freedom to others, deserve it not for themselves."
Abraham Lincoln

Display the character trait for the week:
FAIRNESS

Activity	Materials	Evaluation
Discuss the quote and relate it to fairness. What historical issue do you think prompted President Lincoln to make this statement?	None	Student participation in discussion
Have student groups search the newspaper for articles that illustrate people or groups who are being treated unfairly. Discuss.	Newspapers	Student participation in discussion
Say to students: "I just love brown eyes. I think that today all the brown-eyed people may ignore the no-talking rule during class." After you 'fess up, ask students to talk about how it made them feel. Did any brown-eyed people feel bad? Why?	None	Student participation in discussion
Should famous or important people have to follow the same rules as others? Why or why not?	None	Student participation in discussion
Give student groups illustrative scenarios from yesterday's discussion to act out in role plays.	A prepared role-play suggestion for each group	Participation in planning and performing role plays

GOAL: Student can establish rapport with his/her peer group.

"Sticks in a bundle are unbreakable."

African proverb

Display the character trait for the week:
COOPERATION

Activity	Materials	Evaluation
Take a sheet of paper and tear it in two for the class. Take another and ask a student to fold it in half. Continue letting students fold it until it can't be folded any more. Try to tear it in two. Let students try. Discuss.	Two sheets of paper (any size will do, but it is more dramatic with a large sheet of newsprint or bulletin board paper)	Student participation in discussion
Discuss the quote. Illustrate by holding up a pencil and snapping it in two. Then, hold up several pencils in a bunch and attempt to break them. Let students try too. Are "bundles" of people stronger, too? Discuss.	Pencils	Student participation in discussion
What is cooperation? What do people do when they cooperate? Students work in groups to list examples. Share and discuss.	Chart paper Marker	Student participation in discussion
Are there tasks that one person simply can't do alone? Student groups brainstorm lists of such tasks. Share and discuss.	Paper Pencils	Participation in group work and discussion
Read or tell Aesop's story "The Lion and the Mouse." Discuss how the lion never imagined that a tiny mouse could ever help him. Discuss how people have different talents and strengths and how cooperating to combine them helps the group to succeed where one couldn't.	Summary: A lion catches a mouse, who begs not to be eaten and promises that if freed he will help the lion someday. The lion laughs and frees him. Later, when the lion is caught in a net, the mouse gnaws through the net and frees him.	Student participation in discussion

GOAL: Student respects his/her own personal possessions.

"Never cut what can be untied."
H.Jackson Brown, Life's Little Instruction Book

Display the character trait for the week:
RESPECT

Activity	Materials	Evaluation
Have students work in small groups to open a box tied with string. Allow them to use any method and then show how they got their box open. Be prepared to give a small prize to members of any group that untied the string rather than cutting it.	Empty boxes tied closed with string, prepared beforehand Small prizes	Student participation in the activity and in the discussion
Discuss yesterday's activity, and introduce the quote. Discuss the figurative meaning, eliciting generalization of the concept.	None	Student participation in discussion
Can the quote be applied to our own things? Have students work in small groups to list ways to protect and preserve items on a prepared list. Give an example such as making your bookbag last longer by avoiding overfilling it.	None	Student participation in discussion
Why does the character trait respect go along with this quote? Facilitate a discussion about how respect ties in with caring for and appreciating the things we have.	None	Student participation in discussion
How can we apply this quote to respecting our school? Have small groups work to make posters to promote taking care of school property, such as lockers, books, materials and gym equipment.	Poster board Markers Pencils	Student products and participation in discussion and group activity

GOAL: ## Student respects the personal possessions of others.

"What goes around comes around."

African-American proverb

Display the character trait for the week:
RESPECT

Activity	Materials	Evaluation
Discuss the quote. Relate to the giving and receiving of *respect*. Record as students offer cause/effect examples.	Chart paper headed with RESPECT, with two columns: Cause, Effect Marker	Participation in discussion and brainstorming
Have students work in groups to list ways in which some people fail to respect the personal possessions of others (e.g., stealing, being careless with borrowed items),and make a parallel list of ways we could show respect.	Pencils Paper	Student products
Introduce the idea that supplies and equipment in our school belong to all of us and should be treated with respect. Brainstorm related issues in your school, (e.g., littering, graffiti, misuse of equipment)	Chart paper Marker	Student participation in discussion
Let student groups choose an issue from yesterday's chart with which to do group problem solving. Share and discuss ideas.	Paper Pencils Cards with issues on them from Tuesday	Student products and participation in discussion
Have students work in small groups to write a rap about taking care of others' things. Let each group come up with 2 or 3 lines on a given issue, then put them all together by letting each group "perform" their lines, one after another.	Pencils Paper Cards with issues on them from Tuesday	Participation in rap performances

TEACHING CHARACTER IN THE MIDDLE GRADES

GOAL: # Student exhibits self-discipline.

"Look before you leap."
1350, Oxford Concise Dictionary of Proverbs

Display the character trait for the week:
SELF-DISCIPLINE

Activity	Materials	Evaluation
Pass out drawing paper. Without discussion, ask students to draw a picture to illustrate the quote.	Paper Markers, crayons, colored pencils	Student products
Use student art from yesterday to stimulate discussion of both the literal and figurative meaning of the quote. Review idioms.	Student pictures	Student participation in discussion
Say to the class: "I need a volunteer." When hands go up, choose a student and say, "Thanks. You just agreed to come over to my house later and wash all the windows." After the laughter dies down, ask, "Did he/she look before leaping"?	None	Student participation in discussion
Students often consider the words discipline and punishment synonymous. Discuss and broaden their concept of discipline to one of control.	None	Student participation in discussion
Student groups look for examples in the newspaper of people who have not used self-discipline. Share and discuss.	Newspapers	Participation in small group activity and large group discussion

GOAL: Student exhibits good listening skills.

"A good listener is not only popular everywhere, but after a while, he knows something."

Wilson Mizner

Display the character trait for the week:
RESPECT

Activity	Materials	Evaluation
Take aside a student accomplice before class meeting. Later, call up this student and one other and ask them to role-play two friends. The second student is to tell the first about a movie he/she saw. Your conspirator is going to listen at first, then not pay attention at all. Discuss.	None	Attention to role play and participation in the discussion to follow
All of us need someone who listens. Discuss the quote and have students share in small groups about the person(s) in their lives who fill this need and how they feel about them.	None	Student participation in discussion
Have students write letters or make cards to thank the "listeners" in their lives.	Paper and pencil Markers, crayons, colored pencils Scissors Glue	Student products
Record as students list the rules for good listening (e.g., sit quietly, eyes on speaker, etc.).	Chart paper Marker	Student participation in discussion
How does attentive listening show respect? Review the rules for listening. Ask one side of the class to model poor listening for one minute. Then have the others model good listening. Compare and discuss.	None	Student participation in activity and discussion

GOAL: ## Student works independently.

"It's up to you."
Anonymous

Display the character trait for the week:
RESPONSIBILITY

Activity	Materials	Evaluation
What does independent mean? What does it mean to work independently? Record key words and phrases as students answer.	Chart paper Marker	Student participation in discussion
Give student groups a list of tasks. Reach consensus on each as to whether it can be done independently or not. List on prepared chart paper. Share and discuss.	Markers Chart paper titled INDEPENDENT TASK? with subhead YES and NO for each of the groups	Participation in group activity and discussion
Have student groups discuss the quote, then come back together to compare their interpretations.	None	Student participation in discussion
Relate the quote to larger problems of our community or world. Record as students offer suggested ways for individuals to make a difference in issues like pollution, recycling, etc.	Chart paper Marker	Student participation in discussion
Read the story "One at a Time," from *Chicken Soup for the Soul*, to the class. Discuss.	*Chicken Soup for the Soul* (the original)	Student participation in discussion

GOAL: Student accepts constructive criticism.

"The surest way to lose a friend is to tell him something for his own good."

Sid Ascher

Display the character trait for the week:
GOOD JUDGMENT

Activity	Materials	Evaluation
What is good judgment? Discuss the meaning of the word judge, as both a noun and a verb, and relate it to making choices.	None	Student participation in discussion
Discuss the quote. Have student groups role-play scenarios that involve telling a friend a difficult truth. Discuss.	Prepared cards with scenarios written on them	Student participation in role plays and discussion
Introduce the term *constructive criticism.* Ask students to look up the two words in a dictionary and work in groups to develop a definition for the term. Compare and discuss.	Dictionaries	Student participation in group activity and discussion
One strategy that helps in accepting criticism is "self-talk." Demonstrate and let students practice "think aloud" reactions to sample comments (e.g., If someone says, "You'd make a better grade if you recopied that paper neatly," you "think aloud": "Could that be true? Is this helpful advice?"	Prepared list of constructive comments to make	Student participation in activity
Do role plays in pairs. One student draws a card with a constructive comment written on it. The other responds appropriately.	Prepared cards with comments written on them	Student participation in activity

GOAL: Student plays appropriately with peers.

"Give and take."
1519, Oxford Dictionary of English Proverbs

Display the character trait for the week:
FAIRNESS

Activity	Materials	Evaluation
When kids play games or sports, what kinds of things start arguments? Record as students answer. How many relate to fairness? Discuss why we all want fairness.	Chart paper Marker	Student participation in discussion
Discuss the quote. Look at the list from yesterday. Which items relate to "give and take"?	List from yesterday	Student participation in discussion
Have student groups draw cartoon strips that illustrate "give and take" in games.	Paper Crayons, markers, colored pencils	Student products
Let's talk about the "take" part. Are there times when you should stand and assert yourself on an issue? Talk about appropriate ways to do this. Record as students give examples of positive and negative responses.	Chart paper Marker	Student participation in discussion
Ask students to design T-shirts that advocate fair play. Display in the room.	Paper T-shirt cutouts Pencils Markers	Student products

GOAL: **Student talks appropriately with peers.**

"People must help one another; it is nature's law."

Jean de La Fontaine, Fables

Display the character trait for the week:
KINDNESS

Activity	Materials	Evaluation
How much does what we say affect others? Do you know someone who always says things that make you feel good? Share about that person in small groups.	None	Student participation in discussion
Remember the people we spoke of yesterday. What kinds of things do they say that make us feel so good? Record quotes. Compare and discuss to determine what their common factor is: positive statements. Challenge them to think of a positive response when they don't like the result (e.g., You have really worked hard on this, How great that you finished it!)	Chart paper Marker	Student participation in discussion
Discuss the quote. Have student groups create cartoon strips that show people saying helpful, positive things to others.	Paper Colored pencils, crayons, markers	Student products
Imagine that you overheard a conversation between two others, talking about the kind of friend you are. What would you be proud to hear? Record responses.	Chart paper Marker	Student participation in discussion
Give each a list of students in the class and have them write something positive beside each. Take up and discuss how it felt to do this. Was it difficult or easy? Why? Later, cut and paste each student's comments onto one sheet and return.	Multiple copies of class list	Student participation in discussion

GOAL: ## Student can keep a secret.

"A little leak will sink a big ship."
1616, Dictionary of American Proverbs

Display the character trait for the week:
RESPONSIBILITY

Activity	Materials	Evaluation
Demonstrate the quote using a toy boat and a tub of water. (Test it first!) Discuss how the quote relates to the keeping of secrets? How is telling "just one person" similar to a "small hole"?	Toy boat Tub of water	Student participation in discussion
Invite students to share stories of times when someone did or didn't keep a secret and the result. How did they feel?	None	Student participation in discussion
Discuss secret-keeping from a historical perspective. What kinds of secrets do governments keep from each other? Why? How could this impact history?	None	Student participation in discussion
Secret-keeping is an issue of trust. Is there ever a time when one should break that trust? Record responses and discuss.	Chart paper Marker	Student participation in discussion
Put students into small groups and have each take one scenario from the list of yesterday and develop a simple story. Let reporters from each group tell stories.	Paper Pencils for note taking	Student participation in small-group activity

GOAL: Student expresses affection appropriately.

"Kindness begets kindness."
Sophocles

Display the character trait for the week:
KINDNESS

Activity	Materials	Evaluation
What is *affection*? Lead a discussion that develops a definition, and a list of ways we show affection, and go beyond hugging. Guide students to include the ways we show affection through small acts of kindness.	None	Student participation in discussion
Give students cards, each with one of the ways of showing affection from Monday's list. Read loud from a list of briefly described scenarios and have students hold cards that go with it. Discuss why certain choices were apt or not, why some had more than one match.	Set of prepared cards for each student Prepared list of scenarios (e.g., meeting Mom at the airport, greeting an old friend you haven't seen in a long time, seeing your doctor at a ball game, etc.)	Student participation in activity and discussion
Is it ever appropriate to show affection to strangers, or people you don't know well? Give examples. Have students work in groups to come up with more.	Be ready to give examples, such smiling pleasantly at someone in passing at the post office, holding the door for a mother with a baby, or picking up a package for an older person.	Student participation in smal-group and class discussions
Read and discuss the quote. What does beget mean? What does it mean in this quote? Do you agree?	None	Student participation in discussion
Read or tell "The Smile" from *Chicken Soup for the Soul*. Discuss the small effort and high returns involved in a smile.	A copy of *Chicken Soup for the Soul* (the original)	Attention to the story and participation in the discussion

GOAL: # Student understands the difference between right and wrong.

"What would life be if we had no courage to attempt anything?"

Vincent Van Gogh

Display the character trait for the week:
COURAGE

Activity	Materials	Evaluation
Have students work in small groups to list examples of courage. Have them look for examples in the newspaper. Keep the lists.	Copies of newspaper Paper Pencils	Studnet participation in class and small-group activity
Return yesterday's lists to groups and have reporters read. Guide the discussion to physical vs. moral courage.	Lists from yesterday	Student participation in discussion
Read the quote and discuss. Relate to inventors, artists, and leaders and how they impact society. Why do they need courage?	None	Student participation in discussion
When we are young, our parents teach us and make us do what is right. As we get older, we have to make ourselves do right. Record student examples of times when it takes courage to do the right thing.	Chart paper Marker	Student participation in discussion
Review the list of "right choices" that require courage. Have small groups choose ideas from the list about which to make posters that encourage kids to live a "life of courage."	List from yesterday Poster board Pencils, pens, markers, etc.	Student products

GOAL: ## Student understands the consequences of his/her actions.

"Measure your cloth ten times; you can cut it but once."

Vermont proverb

Display the character trait for the week:
RESPONSIBILITY

Activity	Materials	Evaluation
Define and discuss consequences. You may find that students think of them only in the context of punishment. Ask for positive and negative examples.	None	Student participation in discussion
Revisit Monday's discussion. Have small groups work to make lists of actions and their possible consequences. Share and discuss.	Paper Pencils	Student products and participation in discussion
Explain that you need to wrap a gift quickly before you get started. Begin the wrapping of an empty box and make sure to cut the paper too small. Discuss and relate this to the quote.	Empty box Wrapping paper Scissors	Student participation in discussion
Read the quote again. Have you ever "cut the cloth too quickly"? Sometimes the consequences of acting without thinking carefully can be very serious. Give an example. Record as students brainstorm others.	Chart paper Marker	Student participation in discussion
Post the list from yesterday. Have students work in pairs to make bumper stickers that encourage thinking before we act based on one or more list items.	List from yesterday Paper Pencils, markers	Student products

GOAL: # Student can handle competition.

"To win you have to risk loss."
Jean-Claude Killy

Display the character trait for the week:
COURAGE

Activity	Materials	Evaluation
Ask students to share types of competition they have experience in. Point out that they may compete in things other than sports (e.g, spelling bees, essay contests, fundraisers). Make a graph to illustrate the data.	Chart paper Marker	Participation in sharing info and in making the graph
Refer to yesterday's graph, showing that there is a lot of competition experience in the class. Have students do free writing for ten minutes on winning and losing. Take up the papers and keep.	Graph from yesterday Paper Pencils	Student products
Summarize for the group the general attitudes and beliefs about competition revealed in their writing and discuss. Read the quote and relate it to courage.	None	Student participation in discussion
How can you, as a member of a team in competition, help the team to handle winning and losing in the most productive way? Have small groups plan role plays.	None	Participation in discussion and small-group work
Have students perform the role plays they planned yesterday and discuss.	Any notes or props needed for role plays	Student products and discussion

GOAL: Student has an appropriate sense of humor.

"Laugh and the world laughs with you; weep and you weep alone."

"Solitude," Ella Wheeler Wilcox

Display the character trait for the week:
GOOD JUDGMENT AND KINDNESS

Activity	Materials	Evaluation
Read and discuss the quote. Ask students to draw pictures to illustrate it.	Paper Colored pencils, crayons, markers	Student products
Revisit the quote. Must we always be laughing and cheerful? Of course not. But can we sometimes choose to see the humor in something negative? Give examples. Record student examples.	Chart paper Marker	Student participation in discussion
What place do good judgment and kindness have in a discussion of humor? Have you ever used poor judgment in joking? How did it make others feel? How did you feel?	None	Student participation in discussion
There are different kinds of humor. What appeals to you? Have students name favorite comedians or humorous programs and movies. Discuss what makes them funny (e.g., irony, exaggeration, physical humor).	None	Student participation in discussion
Review the types of humor discussed yesterday. Have students work in small groups to develop cartoon strips based on one type. Share and discuss.	Paper Colored pencils, markers, crayons	Student products

GOAL: Student can adapt to change.

"Who spits against the wind spits in his own face."
1557, Dictionary of American Proverbs

Display the character trait for the week:
COURAGE

Activity	Materials	Evaluation
What are rituals? Give examples and invite students to share about rituals they observe in their families, their churches, this country. Why are rituals important? Rituals create a sense of security born of familiarity and routine.	None	Student participation in discussion
Announce that beginning next school year, the school district lines will be redrawn and the school population split between two schools. After the roar, tell them the truth, that it was just an example. Then ask "Why was this so upsetting? What is it about change that angers and frightens us?" Relate to Monday's discussion.	None	Student participation in discussion
Read and discuss the quote. When a change is beyond our control (e.g., redistricting), what are our choices? Ask small groups to create slogans beginning: "Resisting change is like…"	Paper Pencils	Participation in small group work and discussion
Have small groups discuss the impact of our fear of change on new ideas and inventions in history. Relate it to *courage*. Point out that looking for good things in the change lessens the fear.	Chart paper Marker	Student participation in discussion
Have students draw their own pictures to illustrate the quote.	Paper Colored pencils, crayons, markers	Student products

GOAL: Student controls his/her anger.

"People who fly into a rage always make a bad landing."
Will Rogers

Display the character trait for the week:
SELF-DISCLIPLINE

Activity	Materials	Evaluation
Read and discuss the quote. "Fly into a rage" is an idiom. Compare its literal and idiomatic meanings. Why is it "fly" instead of "stroll" into a rage?	None	Student participation in discussion
Share a personal story of having a bad landing after "flying into a rage." (If you don't have one…good for you!) Ask the students to share their experiences.	None	Student participation in discussion
Record as students brainstorm alternative behaviors when angry (e.g., punching a pillow) or strategies to cool down (e.g., counting, taking deep breaths) before acting.	Chart paper Marker	Student participation in discussion
Give small groups cards with anger-provoking scenarios and have them role-play ways to handle them using strategies from the list.	Index cards with scenarios written on them Behavior list from yesterday	Student participation in planning or performance of role plays
Sometimes anger can fuel positive achievement. In the movie "The Mighty Ducks," the Ducks used their anger and self-discipline at being made fun of and called names to "fire them up" and make them work hard to win. Let students come up, choose a card, read a scenario aloud, and invite ideas from the class on how anger could be channeled productively in that case.	Prepared cards with such scenarios as: Your dad says you can't have a Play Station because your grades are low and you need more study time. Your sister scoffs when you ask her to teach you to play chess and says you are too stupid to learn. You feel angry when you see how many dogs are at the animal shelter.	Student participation in discussion

GOAL: # Student communicates his/her needs appropriately.

"What you don't ask for, you don't get."
Unknown

Display the character trait for the week:
SELF-DISCIPLINE

Activity	Materials	Evaluation
Read and discuss the quote. Have you ever waited for someone to give you what you need, only to find that they didn't know you needed it? Share examples.	None	Student participation in discussion
As we grow, we have different ways of getting what we need. Go through infancy, childhood, teen years and adulthood, and elicit the fact that as one gets older, the means also include earning, trading, and compromise. Record.	Chart paper Marker	Student participation in discussion
Revisit list from yesterday. Where does self-discipline come in? Does crying and screaming work as well for a teenager as it does for a baby? Why or why not?	List from yesterday	Student participation in discussion
Put the class into four groups and assign one of the age ranges to each. Ask them to prepare role-plays to show the most effective way for each to get their needs met. (Be sure to put your class clown in the "infant group"; capitalize on his/her natural talents!)	List from Tuesday	Student participation in small-group planning
It's showtime! Have groups perform role plays.	None	Student participation in role plays and discussion

TEACHING CHARACTER IN THE MIDDLE GRADES

GOAL: # Student respects likenesses and differences in people.

"It's not easy being green."

Kermit the Frog

Display the character trait for the week:
RESPECT AND KINDNESS

Activity	Materials	Evaluation
Revisit an earlier discussion on rituals (week 30). We found that there is a comfort and safety in the familiar sameness. What impact does this have on us when we meet people who are very different from us?	None	Student participation in discussion
Ask students to tell the story of "The Ugly Duckling." The main thrust of this story is about judging others by looks. Can you remember a time when you felt like an "ugly duckling"? Discuss.	None	Student participation in discussion
Read the definitions of *tolerance* and *acceptance*. Why should we try to accept people who are different? Why not just stick with people who are like us? Is this possible?	None	Student participation in discussion
Play or sing Randy Newman's song "Short People." Explain that it was written to make bigoted people think about their own prejudices.	Recording of "Short People" or your own memory	Student participation in discussion and role plays
Build empathy by having groups make posters illustrating different endings to the sentence, "It's not easy being…"	Poster board Pencils, markers	Student products

GOAL: Student recognizes the need to help others.

"Most people are doing the best they can do at any given moment."
Father Joe Coulter

Display the character trait for the week:
KINDNESS

Activity	Materials	Evaluation
Read and discuss the quote. Introduce the idea that even when we've made bad choices or just aren't being at our best, we all need compassion.	None	Student participation in discussion
Can a gesture as small as a smile make a difference? Ask students to make a point to smile at ten different people today and keep a record of their reactions.	None	Student participation in discussion
Make a graph showing the responses to students' smiles.	Prepared graph on poster board, marker	Student participation in completing the graph and in discussion
Read aloud "A Simple Gesture" from *Chicken Soup for the Soul*; discuss.	*Chicken Soup for the Soul* (the original)	Student participation in discussion
The story read yesterday told how a simple gesture of kindness made an impact that saved a life. We never know how the way we treat others, even in small ways, can impact them…so it seems that we should try to treat all with kindness. Ask each to write down one practice that he/she will adopt to do so.	None	Student participation in discussion and student writing

GOAL: Student employs problem-solving techniques.

"Mighty oaks from little acorns grow."

6th century B.C., Lao Tze

Display the character trait for the week:
PERSEVERANCE

Activity	Materials	Evaluation
Review the meaning of perseverance. Record as students name tasks requiring perseverance.	Chart paper Marker	Participation in brain-storming activity
Practice problem-solving in small groups. Give each group one sheet of paper, six paper clips, and three straws. Ask them to make a bridge that can support a Match-box car. Test bridges.	Straws Paper clips Paper Matchbox car	Student cooperation and products
You want to watch a pay-per-view concert on TV. It costs $30 and you don't have the money. Work in small groups to make three or more plans to raise the money. Be creative!	None	Participation in group work
Review ways of giving positive feedback. Then share and evaluate the plans made by groups yesterday. Are they workable?	Plans from yesterday's activities	Participation in discussion
Tell the story of the boy who stopped the leak in the dike with his finger. How does this relate to the quote? Try to think of other examples of one person or group making a big difference.	None	Participation in discussion

GOAL: # Student distinguishes between right and wrong.

"There is no right way to do the wrong thing."
Source unknown

Display the character trait for the week:
HONESTY

Activity	Materials	Evaluation
Sixth graders know the basics of right and wrong. The big issues like stealing are easy. Lying can often enter what seems a gray area. Record as students name kinds of situations in which people lie.	Chart paper Marker	Student participation in discussion
Review list from yesterday. Give a situation to each small group to discuss and reach a consensus.	Paper Pencils	Student participation in group work
Have the reporter for each group share the results of yesterday's discussions. Allow others to comment.	Notes from yesterday	Student participation in discussion
Divide class into two groups. Assign each to prepare to debate one side of the following question: A man who is out of work steals food for his hungry children. Is it wrong? Explain how the debate will proceed.	Paper Pencils	Student participation in group work
Review the rules for the debate and act as the moderator while the two teams present their views.	Set up class so that teams can sit together	Student participation in debate

GOAL: Student participates constructively in school and classroom activities.

"Actions speak louder than words."

Benjamin Franklin, Poor Richard's Almanack

Display the character trait for the week:
CITIZENSHIP

Activity	Materials	Evaluation
Discuss quote. Brainstorm students for their meaning of citizenship (behavior that benefits the common good). Ask what actions might they see others perform in class that demonstrate citizenship.	Chart paper Marker	Student participation in class discussion
Read quote. Discuss appropriate actions that you expect to be seen in the classroom. Choose five rules to focus on during this week. Explain the correct procedure for each ruleand explain their reasons and benefits.	Chart paper Marker	Student participation in class discussion
Review five procedures discussed yesterday. Divide students into five groups. Assign one procedure to each group. Ask students to role-play the correct procedure.	Student responses	Rehearsal of role plays
Allow each group to display their role play of a classroom procedure to the class.	Student demonstrations	Appropriate actions for the procedure
Review five procedures. Discuss the acceptable motivation that an appropriate action displays. Relate to quote and citizenship. How will classroom run smoothly if everyone follows the rules?	Student discussion	Student behavior during discussion

GOAL: Student follows classroom procedures.

"People who are not organized and not ready will suffer the consequences."

Harry Wong

Display the character trait for the week:
RESPONSIBILITY

Activity	Materials	Evaluation
Discuss the quote. How can a student be organized? What tools help that process? What is one consequence of lack of organization?	Chart paper Marker	Student participation in group discussion
Review the quote. What procedures will be used in the classroom for student movement? Discuss what to do when you need a writing tool, when you have finished your work before the others, and when you have a question.	Chart paper Marker	Student participation in group discussion
Review yesterday's procedures. Ask for a volunteer to demonstrate how to perform that procedure. Allow the class to rehearse that action several times.	Yesterday's list	Student participation in group discussion
Discuss new procedures for what to do when you need the restroom, when you are going to be absent and when you will be dismissed from class.	Chart paper Marker	Student participation in group discussion
Review yesterday's procedures. Ask for a volunteer to demonstrate how to perform that procedure. Allow the class to rehearse that action several times. Relate to being organized and avoiding consequences.	Yesterday's list	Student participation in group discussion

GOAL: # Student participates constructively in making group decisions.

"All people have equal choices to be cooperative and dependable."

Donna B. Forrest

Display the character trait for the week:
RESPONSIBILITY

Activity	Materials	Evaluation
Discuss the quote. Why do we have procedures? Why is it important to know acceptable ways to do things? How are procedures important in a student's daily activities? Cite last two weeks' work on procedures.	None	Student participation in group discussion
Review last week's discussion of classroom procedures that were developed. Discuss their effectiveness in the classroom. Vote to keep the ones that are working. Save the rest for tomorrow.	List of procedures from last week Chart paper Marker	Student participation in group discussion
Review yesterday's procedures that are working. Discuss the ones that are not working. Vote to discard or amend. Redesign the procedures that will promote a smooth-running classroom.	Chart paper Marker	Student participation in group discussion
Allow class group to make decisions on the following routines: days of tests, use of free homework passes, and rewards for achievement. What other new decisions could the group make for the good of the class?	Chart paper Marker	Student participation in group discussion
Discuss established procedures. When done right, what will class do to give feedback? Design a suggestion box for ideas for group decisions.	Shoebox Paper to cover it Tape Markers	Suggestion box completed

GOAL: # Student assumes responsibility for routine activities.

"You cannot escape the responsibilities of tomorrow by evading them today."
E.C. McKenzie

Display the character trait for the week:
RESPONSIBILITY

Activity	Materials	Evaluation
Discuss the quote. Cite instances of things that all 7th graders do. What classroom procedure is everyone expected to use? How is this going in our classroom? Commend class on appropriate use in the classroom.	Procedures list	Student participation in group discussion
Fold a piece of paper into four parts. Label parts: Me Alone, Me with Others, Me with Friends, Me with My Teacher. Describe a way that you take responsibility.	Paper Pen or pencil	Individual responses on paper
Share responses from yesterday's writing. Allow students to discuss ways to show responsibility.	Student papers	Student participation in group discussion
Who likes to be nagged (about doing homework, picking up clothes, etc)? Discuss how responsibility is using correct procedures in various situations. When you do the procedure correctly, the nagging stops.	None	Student participation in group discussion
Discuss quote. Cite incidences that students have used the correct procedure to accomplish a task in the classroom or community. Commend students on the use.	None	Student participation in group discussion

GOAL: ## Student exhibits appropriate behaviors for different environments.

"One leg cannot dance alone."

East African proverb

Display the character trait for the week:
RESPONSIBILITY

Activity	Materials	Evaluation
Discuss the quote as related to developing responsibility. Who are some of the people on whom we rely? For what?	Chart paper Markers	Student participation in group discussion
Assign one environment to each group: library, halls, lunchroom, restroom, bus. Allow groups to brainstorm what rules they might need to use in these areas. What benefit do we derive from everyone following the rules? Assign students to work in groups.	Paper Pens or pencils	Small-group participation
Discuss the rules that each group has listed. Narrow the list down to three rules in each environment. Groups must agree on their choices.	List from yesterday Markers	Small-group participation
Class discusses rules for each area. Ask a volunteer to make a poster of the rules. Keep it visible for all to see.	List from yesterday Markers	Small-group participation
Designate one person from each group to role-play correct use of the rules for each environment. How does responsible behavior affect our relationships with others, as the quote implies?	List from yesterday Markers	Student participation in group discussion

GOAL: # Student recognizes the need for fair rules and laws.

"Ignorance of the law excuses no man."
John Selden

Display the character trait for the week:
CITIZENSHIP

Activity	Materials	Evaluation
Discuss quote. What are laws that students must obey while on school property? How do we learn about them? Do they seem fair? What are their benefits? Relate to citizenship as a duty to be informed.	Chart paper Markers	Student participation in group discussion
Discuss delinquent behavior. List several: bringing weapons to school, destroying property, inflicting injury. Discuss reasons for such behavior. What is a citizen's obligation to community when faced with delinquent behavior?	Chart paper Markers	Student participation in group discussion
List school personnel to whom students could report a broken school law and how they should report. Suggest a "Safe Schools" box where students can deposit notes to principal.	List Markers	Student participation in group discussion
Refer to Tuesday's list of behaviors. How can delinquent behavior be prevented? List how one can accept responsibility (e.g., apologizing, making amends, choosing alternate behavior).	List Chart paper Markers	Student participation in group discussion
Discuss the quote as it applies to 7th graders. What rules are easier to follow? What consequences are established for delinquent behavior? What is our obligation as citizens of the school or community?	List Markers	Student participation in group discussion

GOAL: Student assumes responsibility for his/her actions.

"Responsibility is the price of greatness."
Winston Churchill

Display the character trait for the week:
RESPONSIBILITY

Activity	Materials	Evaluation
Discuss quote. How do we take responsibility for our actions? What kind of actions?	None	Student participation in group discussion
Divide class into small groups of four. Ask them to list one time that they have violated a rule at home or school. What were the consequences?	Paper Pens or pencils	Small-group participation
Refer to yesterday's list. Swap lists with other groups. Suggest alternate behaviors that the student could have used instead of breaking a rule.	Yesterday's lists Pens or pencils	Small-group participation
Using previous lists of violations, develop an appropriate restitution for each behavior: admitting wrongdoing, apologizing, performing, restitution.	Yesterday's lists Pens or pencils	Small-group participation
Read lists of restitutions developed to demonstrate how students can take responsibility for their actions.	Yesterday's lists	Student responses to suggestions

GOAL: Student shows respect for authority figures.

"Experience is not what happens to you.
It is what you do with what happens to you."
Aldous Huxley

Display the character trait for the week:
RESPECT

Activity	Materials	Evaluation
Show the relationship between the experiences of learning to the wisdom of authority figures. Who are the authority figures in the school. How did they achieve their status?	None	Student participation in group discussion
List areas where we encounter authority figures: home, school, community, court, stores. What positions do these people hold?	Chart papers Markers	Student participation in group discussion
Brainstorm ways to show appreciation and support for people in authority.	Lists Pens or pencils	Student participation in group discussion
Using yesterday's lists, discuss obstacles to following directions from authority. How can students display acceptance of authority? What would the procedure be? Practice: Look, stay calm, use a pleasant voice, say "OK" in response.	Lists	Student participation in group discussion
Review the quote again. How does respecting authority affect what happens to you? Give examples.	None	Student participation in group discussion

GOAL: ## Student can analyze classroom problems and come up with solutions.

"Growing up is only the understanding that one's unique, incredible experience is what everyone shares."

Author unknown

Display the character trait for the week
COOPERATION

Activity	Materials	Evaluation
Discuss the meaning of the quote and how it applies to students. What common experiences do 7th graders share, both physically and emotionally?	None	Student participation in group discussion
Ask students to name the school difficulties they have (e.g., teacher doesn't like them, no time to study). Choose the five problems that tend to occur most frequently.	Chart paper Markers	Student participation in group discussion
Review list of five problems. Divide class into five groups. Assign one problem to each group. List three possible solutions for each. Explain how these might work well in any classroom.	Chart paper Markers	Small-group participation
Share solutions with whole class. Show how to perform the new solution (e.g., the better way to explain something to a teacher) so that all will understand what the replacement behavior should resemble.	Yesterday's list	Class presentations
Class can vote on the most appropriate solution to use as a new procedure. Rehearse and refine as the new expectation for behavior.	List of solutions	Student participation in group discussion

GOAL: Student establishes rapport with his/her peer group.

"The only way to have a friend is to be one."
Ralph Waldo Emerson

Display the character trait for the week:
KINDNESS

Activity	Materials	Evaluation
Have students look up *rapport* in dictionary and discuss its meaning. List synonyms. Examine the quote as describing rapport in action.	Chart paper Market	Student participation in group discussion
Each student writes his/her name at the top of a piece of paper. Divide the paper in half by folding it vertically. Pass the paper to the person to the right., who will write something positive about the person named at the top in the left column and sign his/her name in the right. Continue to pass the papers until all students have made an entry on each paper.	Lined paper Pens or pencils	Individual responses on paper
Allow students time to quietly read all student responses. Ask for volunteers to read their lists.	Yesterday's lists	Student participation in group discussion
Discuss the effects of reading positive statements about yourself. How did you feel when you read a comment that you did not anticipate? How can positive statements increase our rapport with our peers?	Yesterday's lists	Student participation in group discussion
Review quote and meaning of rapport. How can we show that we appreciate each other on a daily basis? What kinds of statements can we make to increase our appreciation of others?	None	Student participation in group discussion

GOAL: Students recognizes likenesses and differences in people.

"It won't make any difference a hundred years from now."

Anonymous—cited by Louis Berman

Display the character trait for the week:
ACCEPTANCE

Activity	Materials	Evaluation
Discuss quote. Why is "100 years" a significant number? How do we accept or reject people? Ask them to tell of instances when they disliked someone, then later learned to like that person. What happened?	None	Student participation in group discussion
Divide class into pairs. Allow 5 minutes for students to list similarities that they share. Allow another 5 minutes to list differences that they have from each other.	Paper Pens or pencils	Small group participation
Discuss categories on yesterday's lists. How can we notice and appreciate the special features of each other? Why will this make no difference 100 years from now?	Lists	Student participation in group discussion
Refer to social studies textbook. Choose any country to examine. List three similarities and three differences between that society and ours.	Social studies textbook Paper Pens or pencils	Completed lists from individual students
Use yesterday's lists. How would a person from that country be accepted in the U.S.? How would we accept that person into our classroom?	Student lists	Student participation in group discussion

GRADE
7
WEEK
12

GOAL: Student empathizes with others.

"One kind action is better than a thousand kind thoughts."
Author unknown

Display the character trait for the week:
KINDNESS

Activity	Materials	Evaluation
Differentiate between *sympathy* and *empathy*. (You can sympathize with a friend's loss of her dog though you've never had a dog; you can empathize with a friend's being cut from a team if it has also happened to you.) Give examples in the classroom when we might empathize with each other.	Dictionary Book of Synonyms	Student participation in group discussion
Discuss quote. How is kindness related to empathy? What is the difference between having a kind thought and doing a kind action? Thoughts stay in a person's head unless they are expressed in an action. List three kind actions and three kind thoughts you could say when action isn't possible ("Sorry you have to move away.")	None	Student participation in group discussion
How can students make the classroom a better place? Divide class into small groups. List ways to show compassion for others in the classroom, lunchroom, hallways, library, bus.	Chart paper Makers	Small group participation Completed posters
Discuss lists from yesterday. Share ideas. How can we help others because we care? Is telling or showing better?	Lists from yesterday	Student participation in group discussion
Empathy can be used in other areas of our lives. Give several examples. When could you show kindness at home, in sports, at the store, in the community?	Chart paper Markers	Student participation in group discussion

GOAL: # Student recognizes examples of community service.

"Lose no time. Be always employed at something useful. Cut off all unnecessary actions."

Benjamin Franklin

Display the character trait for the week:
COOPERATION

Activity	Materials	Evaluation
Discuss quote. Define *employed* and tell how a student is usefully employed at the 7th grade level. What's the value of it? What unnecessary actions do we perform?	None	Student participation in group discussion
Distribute poster paper to student groups. Title: We can work together in the community. List tasks that a student can do to offer a service within the community.	Poster paper Markers	Small-group participation
Using yesterday's lists, share with whole class. How must we be ready and willing to work with others toward a common intention? When are we available to perform these services?	Yesterday's posters Markers	Small-group participation
Review lists of community services that were suggested yesterday. Who are people in the community we can contact to offer our services as a helper? How can we access these agencies or neighbors?	Yesterday's posters Markers Telephone book	Student participation in group discussion
Review several community tasks that have been suggested. What's the best way to tackle an unpleasant task, such as cleaning up a rundown play area? How might students feel after helping someone?	Poster lists	Student participation in group discussion

GOAL: # Student distinguishes between wants and needs.

"You can't always get what you want."
Rolling Stones

Display the character trait for the week:
SELF-DISCIPLINE

Activity	Materials	Evaluation
Discuss quote. Begin two lists labeled "Wants" and "Needs." What are 10 things that a 7th grader wants? What are 10 things that a 7th grader needs? (Ask if any wants from last year are now not important.)	Chart paper Markers	Student participation in group discussion
Examine yesterday's lists of wants to determine the most important items. Renumber from one to ten, using class consensus. Do the same for needs. Cross off the ones that you cannot have nor obtain. How are wants different from needs?	Yesterday's lists Quote	Student participation in group discussion
Ask students to tell about a prized possession and why it is important to them. Is it a true need or just a want? Could you live without it?	None	Student participation in group discussion
Use social studies textbook to choose a foreign country. Generate a list of wants and needs that a person living there might have.	Social studies textbook Paper Pens or pencils	Individual lists from each student
Use yesterday's lists. How are our wants and needs different from other students'? What happens when a need is replaced by a want?	Yesterday's lists	Student participation in group discussion

GOAL: # Student can predict the consequences of responsible and irresponsible actions.

"What a man sows, so shall he reap."

Galatians 6:7

Display the character trait for the week:
GOOD JUDGMENT

Activity	Materials	Evaluation
Discuss quote. Define reaping and sowing. How is reaping what we have sown like predicting what will happen because of our actions?	Chart paper Marker	Student participation in group discussion
We know to obey our parents and be responsible to them. Give several examples of being responsible at home. What will happen to us as a result of each action?	Chart paper Marker	Student participation in group discussion
Give several examples of showing irresponsible behavior at home. What will be the consequences for each of these actions?	Chart paper Marker	Student participation in group discussion
Review list of irresponsible behaviors. How can we predict the results of mature, responsible behavior? Who will be affected by it? Demonstrate how to stop, think, and evaluate our responses. Suggest alternatives for irresponsible behaviors on the list.	Yesterday's list Chart paper Marker	Student participation in group discussion
Share memories of when you have witnessed unpredictable behavior (a temper tantrum, sudden laughing aloud, a frightening response). Predict what the outcome will be if you use that action now. Will it be acceptable? What behavior will you use to replace it?	None	Student participation in group discussion

GOAL: ## Student can explain the need to apply rules fairly.

"No man is above the law and no man is below it; nor do we ask any man's permission when we require him to obey it."
Theodore Roosevelt

Display the character trait for the week:
FAIRNESS

Activity	Materials	Evaluation
Discuss quote. How do we use rules to work in different ways? (No loud talk in halls, but it's OK to yell at someone about to fall down stairs.) Are the same rules good for school and home? Give an example.	None	Student participation in group discussion
Divide students into groups of four. Assign a recorder. Each student will tell one family rule and the reason and benefit for that rule. Take turns until each student has contributed three rules.	Paper Markers	Small-group participation Completed lists
Review lists of rules. Are these rules fair for every member in the family? (For girls and boys? for all ages?) Why not? Tell the age of the family member and reason why the rule would not apply fairly.	Yesterday's list on paper Markers	Small-group participation
Brainstorm for a list of rules that would apply to 7th graders but not to elementary-age children. Why would it be unfair to impose these rules on a younger group? Why would these rules be fair for an older group?	Chart paper Marker	Student participation in group discussion
Review list of rules from Tuesday. How can a rule be applied differently in sports, during leisure time, or in school. Give examples.	Tuesday's list	Student participation in group discussion

GOAL: **Student respects his/ her own personal possessions.**

"These are a few of my favorite things."

Oscar Hammerstein

Display the character trait for the week:
RESPECT

Activity	Materials	Evaluation
Discuss quote as a verse from a popular song. Ask each student to name one item that is his or her favorite item and write it on an index card. Tell when and how they received it.	Index cards Pencils	Completed index cards
Review yesterday's cards. Add how you take care of your item. Where do you store it? Do you allow anyone else to use it? Why is taking acare of one's possessions important at any age?	Index cards from yesterday Pencils	Completed index cards Student cooperation
Swap index cards with a nearby student. Read that card. On the back tell how this item would be of value to you and how you would protect it. Return card to owner. Were there differences? Why?	Yesterday's index cards Pencils	Completed index cards
Review index cards. Tell how you would feel if you lost your possession or if it were damaged. Would you be able to replace it? How could you have prevented the problem?	Yesterday's index cards	Student participation in group discussion
List some general rules about how to take care of personal possessions? Would you share your possessions with others? Do you still have items that you have kept since you were a baby?	Chart paper Marker	Student participation in group discussion

GOAL: # Student respects the personal possessions of others.

"By taking care of the property of others, there is less room for disagreements."

Donna B. Forrest

Display the character trait for the week:
RESPECT

Activity	Materials	Evaluation
Discuss quote. Why should we respect the property of others? (We didn't pay for them, they may have special meaning) How would this prevent disagreements?	Chart paper Marker	Student participation in group discussion
Fold a piece of paper into 3 columns. Label the top of each column with school, home and work. List some personal possessions that one would have at school, in the home, at work?	Paper Marker	Small-group participation
Review yesterday's list. How would you recognize that these belonged to someone else? How could you obtain one of these possessions and show respect for it?	List of possessions	Student participation in group discussion
Look at the list of personal possessions. Imagine that you lost or failed to return one item to the owner. Demonstrate how you'd explain its disappearance and your plan to replace it. How do you think the owner would feel?	Yesterday's list of possessions	Student participation in group discussion
Describe the classroom procedure for borrowing and using materials that belong to the teacher or to other students. How can you show respect for that property? List ways.	Chart paper Marker	Student participation in group discussion

GOAL: Student exhibits self-control.

"Who is powerful? He that governs his passions."

Benjamin Franklin

Display the character trait for the week:
SELF-DISCIPLINE

Activity	Materials	Evaluation
Discuss quote. What does it mean to govern your passions? Why would that make you powerful?	Dictionary	Student participation in group discussion
Divide into small groups. Choose one behavior that shows lack of self-control that has happened in the classroom, school, and bus. Develop a replacement behavior that should have been displayed.	Paper Pens or pencils	Small-group participation
Divide into small groups. List three times when it was difficult to show self-control and you almost lost your ability to do the right thing. How did you handle the situation?	Paper Pencils	Small-group participation
Look in your literature book for a character who demonstrated self-control. Discuss circumstances and the result.	None	Small-group participation
Look in the newspaper for reports of people who acted without self-control. What could the person have done differently to show self-discipline? Can you find any articles about people who did show self-discipline?	Daily newspaper	Student participation in group discussion

GOAL: Student exhibits good listening skills.

"A moment's insight is sometimes worth a life's experience."
Oliver Wendell Holmes

Display the character trait for the week:
SELF-DISCIPLINE

Activity	Materials	Evaluation
Discuss quote. Give examples of having enough insight to remain silent and not interrupt.	None	Student participation in group discussion
Demonstrate the skill of listening to class: 1) Look at the person speaking. 2) Listen to what the person is saying. 3) Remain quiet, no interrupting. 4) Repeat what the person is saying, to yourself, silently. 5) Summarize. Allow students to practice while teacher reads a brief paragraph.	None	Class attention Student participation
Divide class into pairs. One student will read a short passage. The other will listen. Use the five steps to listen.	Literature book	Student participation in pairs
Design a poster with pictures to show what each listening skill resembles: eyes watching, ears listening, mouth closed, body quiet.	Poster Markers	Student participation in small groups
Develop a class signal to use to cue others to listen when they are interrupting. Rehearse the cue with one person interrupting and one person giving the nonverbal signal.	None	Student participation in pairs

GOAL: Student works independently.

"Ideas of youth are the foundation of creation."

Dolores Z. Justin

Display the character trait for the week:
SELF-DISCIPLINE

Activity	Materials	Evaluation
Discuss quote. Many good ideas may be generated in group brainstorming, but how do we develop ideas when working independently? When can you work on your own and be creative?	None	Student participation in group discussion
Divide class into small groups. Discuss strategies that would make working alone more pleasant when doing homework, such as work for several short intervals, take a 5-minute snack break or stretch time, set a timer, set a deadline for completion. Ask students to try it tonight.	Paper Pencils	Small-group participation Completed lists
Review strategies in small groups. Ask students how successful they were doing homework independently last night. Share ideas. What made the experience more effective?	Yesterday's lists	Small-group participation
Cite differences between working with others and alone. What does a student look like who is working quietly and on task? List ideas and demonstrate in the classroom.	Chart paper Marker	Student participation in group discussion
How can we complete a task without being directed? How can we follow through on a task without losing concentration? What are some home activities that can be done independently?	Chart paper Marker	Student participation in group discussion

GOAL: Student accepts constructive criticism.

"A true critic ought to dwell rather upon excellencies than imperfections."
Joseph Addison

Display the character trait for the week:
SELF-DISCIPLINE

Activity	Materials	Evaluation
Differentiate between constructive and destructive criticism. Give several examples of criticism, asking class to decide if they are constructive or destructive. What makes the difference?	Dictionary	Student participation in group discussion
Discuss quote. Make a list of the good things you have seen students do. Did anyone congratulate the person who performed well? Practice telling someone how well they have done something today by citing things that were appealing.	Chart paper Marker	Student participation in group discussion
Discuss how you might offer someone criticism to improve something (e.g., a sports skill, the condition of work handed in, need for mouthwash). Demonstrate how to accept criticism: Look at the person offering criticism, say "OK," no arguing, say "Thank you." Have students role-play.	Yesterday's lists	Student participation in group discussion
Focus on having a good attitude about accepting criticism. Use positive language to make a point. With a partner, review the procedure for accepting criticism.	Yesterday's lists	Small-group rehearsal
Offer a criticism. Ask for five volunteers to accept it nicely.	None	Student participation in group discussion

GOAL: ## Student plays appropriately with his/her peer group.

"What all men are really after is some form, or perhaps only some formula, of peace."

Joseph Conrad

Display the character trait for the week:
COOPERATION

Activity	Materials	Evaluation
Discuss quote. How can peace result from appropriate play?	None	Student participation in group discussion
List what games a 7th grader plays. What activities are used? Consider games at school and at home.	Index cards Markers	Student participation in group discussion
Review lists. How can we play in an acceptable manner? Suggest: 1) Follow rules of the game. 2) Decide what each person will do. 3) Share items of the game. 4) Praise the efforts of others. 5) Stay calm and relaxed. Demonstrate using two volunteers in a pretend card game.	Chart paper Markers	Student participation in group discussion
Review procedure for interacting with others appropriately. Rehearse in small groups. Choose a typical game to role-play the procedure.	Wednesday's lists	Student participation in group discussion
Discuss appropriate techniques for cooperative recreation time. Discuss what frustrations you might experience during a game. How can you figure out what causes the frustration? How can you walk away from a game?	Wednesday's lists of procedures	Student participation in group discussion

GOAL: Student talks appropriately with his/her peer group.

"If you haven't got anything nice to say about a person, don't say anything at all."
Mother's admonition

Display the character trait for the week:
GOOD JUDGMENT

Activity	Materials	Evaluation
Discuss quote. What kind of conversation makes people feel good? What good will "saying nothing" do?	None	Student participation in group discussion
List words that are kind to use with conversation. List words that are harmful to others' feelings. Give some examples of how these words will affect others.	Chart paper Marker	Student participation in group discussion
On a piece of paper, ask students to write a harmful putdown that he has heard. Tell why it hurt. Share with class.	Index cards Markers	Completed index cards Student participation
Using yesterday's index cards, review the responses. Tear up each card into small pieces and throw in trash. What does this symbolize?	Yesterday's index cards Trash can	Student participation Eliminated index cards.
Demonstrate acceptable volume and tone for speaking appropriately to peers, according to the environment. Does place and time influence how we share conversation with our peers? Give examples.	None	Student participation in group discussion

GOAL: ## Student can keep a secret.

"Conversation would be vastly improved by the constant use of four simple words: I do not know."

Andre Maurois

Display the character trait for the week:
HONESTY

Activity	Materials	Evaluation
Discuss quote. Why say "I do not know" rather than tell the secret? What makes a secret confidential? Has anyone been hurt by a friend telling your confidential information?	None	Student participation in group discussion
Distribute materials to five volunteers. Have them come up to a front table that can be viewed by all. Tell students to squirt a small amount of paste onto the paper. Next, ask each student to put the paste back into the tube they are holding. How does this symbolize what happens to a secret once it is told? We can't take back our words after speaking them.	5 small tubes of colorful toothpaste 5 small squares of construction paper	Student participation
Review yesterday's activity. How does telling a secret represent the paste on the paper? The little dabs that would not fit back into the tube remained on the paper. This represents how distorted words can become. The stain on the back of the paper shows how deep the hurt is.	None	Student participation in group discussion
Review the quote. How does this relate to the paste activity? Would it have been easier to just keep the paste in the tube?	None	Student participation in group discussion
When is it acceptable to tell a secret and to whom? Would trust be broken?	None	Student participation in group discussion

GOAL: Student expresses affection appropriately.

"Don't tell me no lies and keep your hands to yourself."
Georgia Satellites

Display the character trait for the week:
GOOD JUDGMENT

Activity	Materials	Evaluation
Define affection and give three synonyms. How can affection be expressed? What words are acceptable? How about a smile and a helping hand?	Dictionary Chart paper Marker	Student participation in group discussion
Discuss quote. What persuasion might be told to persuade a person to allow themselves to be touched inappropriately? Discuss how our bodies are our own and private, not to be invaded by others. Can students suggest one of their songs to cite complaints about touching?	Song suggestions	Student participation in group discussion
When is it inappropriate to put a hand on another person? How can you ask the person if it is OK to touch them? Are hugs acceptable in school? What touching is allowed in school?	None	Student participation in group discussion
Design a symbol or drawing to express affection appropriately. Use positive, acceptable language and ideas.	Paper Markers	Individual projects
Practice talking for three minutes to a partner without placing hands on the person. Did you tend to tap the person on the shoulder or the arm? Rehearse using appropriate words to express feelings in a kind manner.	None	Individual responses in small group discussion

GOAL: Student understands the difference between right and wrong.

"Crime does not pay."
Slogan of the FBI

Display the character trait for the week:
GOOD JUDGMENT

Activity	Materials	Evaluation
Discuss quote. Give examples of actions that are right and some that are wrong.	None	Student participation in group discussion
Look for reports of criminal actions. What made them offensive? What could the person have done differently?	Daily newspaper	Small-group participation
Have students write "No Excuses" at the top of an index card, then list actions that are wrong. Instead of offering an excuse, what could a student do to show correct behavior?	Index cards Pencils	Small-group participation
In small groups, list some wrongdoing that occurs at school. Brainstorm for ideas to remedy the situations. What would you do in that case? Why were the actions wrong?	Paper Pencils	Small-group participation
Review some rights and wrongs discussed this week. What makes things right or wrong? How do we learn the difference?	Wednesday's and Thursday's lists	Student participation in group discussion

GOAL: Student understands the consequences of his/ her actions.

"Many a man's tongue broke his nose."
Seamus MacManus

Display the character trait for the week:
SELF-DISCIPLINE

Activity	Materials	Evaluation
Discuss character trait and relate to the goal. What are consequences? Why is being honest about our actions important? Are there always bad consequences for our actions? Pick an action and list both bad and good ones.	Chart paper Marker	Student participation in group discussion
Discuss the quote. Give examples of times when words have brought about negative reactions. What were the consequences? How could those words have been restated or avoided?	None	Student participation in group discussion
Look at examples of war in the social studies textbook. List a consequence that was cited. How did a group take responsibility for its actions?	Social studies textbook Paper Pen or pencil	Small-group discussion
Discuss problem behaviors that typically happen in the classroom. Assign two problems to each group. What results will occur because of the behavior? Develop responses that the students can use to show that they have understood and accepted the consequences.	Paper Pens or pencils	Small-group participation
Review several scenarios that were discussed yesterday. State the acceptance of the consequences. What good consequences could have resulted?	Yesterday's lists	Student participation in group discussion

GOAL: Student can handle competition.

"Success isn't necessarily permanent— but neither is failure."

E.C. McKenzie

Display the character trait for the week:
COOPERATION

Activity	Materials	Evaluation
What is competition? When do we compete? List several activities besides sports that involve competition at school and at home.	None	Student participation in large group discussion
Discuss quote. How do we feel when we have been successful? When we have experienced failure? How long did it take for those feelings to go away?	None	Large or small-group discussion.
Use sports section of local daily newspaper. List examples of competition that were successful and those that were failures. Look for statements that told how the players felt. Would anything have been accomplished without teamwork?	Daily local newspaper	Small-group participation
When is competition healthy? List some benefits. When is competition dangerous? List examples.	Paper Pencils or pens	Small-group participation
Using yesterday's lists, discuss events in students' own lives in which they compete. Have they ever felt like giving up? What kind of teamwork did they use? What did they accomplish that made them feel successful? Was competition comfortable?	Yesterday's lists	Student participation in group discussion

GOAL: Student uses an appropriate sense of humor.

"The best sense of humor belongs to the person who can laugh at himself."
Old proverb

Display the character trait for the week:
JOYFULNESS

Activity	Materials	Evaluation
Discuss quote. When do we have the opportunity to laugh at ourselves? What is humor?	None	Student participation in group discussion
How many types of humor can you identify? List them (e.g., puns, limericks, comic strips, jokes, stand-up comedy, plays, songs, pictures). With which are you most familiar? What makes them funny?	Paper Pen or pencil	Student participation in group discussion
Give examples of humor that is appropriate. Give examples of humor that is hurtful or harmful. How can we judge the difference?	None	Student participation in group discussion
Interjecting humor can lighten a difficult situation. What could you say, using humor, to make someone laugh who has just failed a test, or is about to perform a difficult task?	None	Small-group participation
Using your own favorite type of humor, write an example. Share with the group. Was it appropriate or harmful? Could you change it to be acceptable?	Paper Pen or pencil	Small-group participation

GOAL: ## Student can adapt to change.

"Courage is not the absence of fear, but the conquest of it."

E. C. McKenzie

Display the character trait for the week:
COURAGE

Activity	Materials	Evaluation
Discuss the goal and what it means to adapt. Who's had a family change recently (e.g., new baby, new house). How long did it take to get used to? What made you feel better during transition?	None	Student participation in group discussion
Define *courage*. It doesn't always mean battlefield heroics, but can be merely having a good attitude while doing something difficult, like moving to new town. Relate that to the quote. What is a conquest? What happens to fear when you act courageously?	None	Student participation in group discussion
Discuss famous people who rose to greatness during a time of change or crisis (e.g., Lincoln, Churchill, anyone who rescues another). They had courage to act boldly in their beliefs, even when opposed by other people.	Chart paper Marker	Individual participation in small, cooperative group
Using yesterday's lists, tell how the actions of these people being courageous affected others around them and created a ripple effect. How did people involved have to adapt to change?	Yesterday's papers Markers	Small-group participation
Is change good or bad? List three good and three bad changes. Discuss how bad changes can have good elements (e.g., having to ride the bus to school lets you make a new friend, having a bike stolen makes you take care of your things.)	Paper Pens or pencils	Small-group participation

GOAL: Student controls his/her anger.

"It was a terrible, horrible, no good, very bad day."
Judith Viorst

Display the character trait for the week:
SELF-DISCIPLINE

Activity	Materials	Evaluation
What makes us get angry? Describe physical symptoms (e.g., red face, pounding heart). They're natural, but what results does expressing anger get us? Discuss the character trait and how controlling anger until symptoms pass can help you get more of what you want .	None	Student participation in group discussion
Look at the quote and discuss goal. Using a dictionary or thesaurus, list synonyms for "anger." Make a list of how anger is expressed.	Dictionary, thesaurus Paper Pen or pencil	Small group participation
Look at the ways that anger is expressed on yesterday's lists. Next to each, devise a replacement behavior or expression that could be substituted for the angry response. Practice this in role plays.	Yesterday's lists	Small-group participation One volunteer from each group performs role play
Discuss events in a school day that would make a student feel angry. What type of self-discipline would one need to control that anger? List strategies people use to let the anger pass (e.g., counting, deep breathing).	Chart paper Marker	Student participation in group discussion
Devise ways to use anger control in the classroom. Designate a private Time Out space in the room where a student can retreat when needing to escape for a short time period to regain self-control. Develop a signal to use. Review to practice procedure.	Poster paper Marker Sign for "Time Out" Chair for "Time Out"	Student participation in group discussion

GOAL: Student communicates his/her needs appropriately.

"One way to get along better in the world is to be just a little kinder than necessary."

Dr. Judith Brandt

Display the character trait for the week:
KINDNESS

Activity	Materials	Evaluation
Discuss the goal. In what ways do we "communicate"? What are some needs that we have to have met in school, at home, in the community?	None	Student participation in group discussion Each student gives one example of his or her "need"
Pretend that you cannot speak. Practice an acceptable way to request to sharpen your pencil, use the restroom, go to the nurse, get help on your homework, get a drink of water.	None	Cooperative participation in small group situation.
Everyone expresses feelings in a different manner. Review yesterday's topics to make each request using kind words that express an acceptable feeling. How did it feel to communicate your need with kindness? Was it difficult?	Yesterday's topics	Small-group participation
Practice expressing needs appropriately. 1) Think about the need or the situation. 2) Monitor that feeling that you have and name it. 3) Breathe deeply to relax at this time. 4) Calmly describe your need and feeling to someone. 5) Praise yourself when you say it calmly and kindly.	Yellow or gold cards with five steps preprinted clearly	Small-group participation with individual role play
When students communicate appropriately, learning is easier. Give five examples that use classroom procedures to resolve a need.	List of classroom procedures	Student participation in group discussion Volunteers to role-play communication of procedure

GOAL: Student solves problems in a peaceful way.

"Give peace a chance."
John Lennon & Paul McCartney

Display the character trait for the week:
PERSEVERANCE

Activity	Materials	Evaluation
Play the recording. What does the quote mean? Define perseverance. Why does it take perseverance to use peaceful methods?	Recording of Beatles' "Give Peace a Chance."	Student participation in group discussion
Fold a piece of paper into three sections. In one part, write a conflict that has occurred with another classmate. In the second part, write a typical 7th grader's response. In the third part, write a peaceful solution to resolve it.	Paper Pen or pencil	Individual participation. Completion of three-sectioned paper
Exchange yesterday's papers. In pairs, try the solution. If it worked to resolve the problem, write "Yes" at the top of the third section. If it didn't work, write "No." Write suggestions.	Yesterday's papers	Small groups of paired students
Use same procedure with three-sectioned paper. This time use examples of a conflict that occurred in the home.	Paper Pen or pencil	Individual participation Completion of 3 sectioned paper
Read or play a tape of "I Have a Dream" by Dr. Martin Luther King. What conflicts did he experience? How did he work to offer a peaceful solution? How can you work to solve problems in your own neighborhood?	Recording or written excerpts of speech	Individual attention to recording Student participation in group discussion

GOAL: Student demonstrates a positive attitude.

"No act of kindness, no matter how small, is ever wasted."

Aesop

Display the character trait for the week:
KINDNESS

Activity	Materials	Evaluation
Discuss character trait and goal. Attitude is what we make it, good or bad. How can people influence our attitude?	None	Student participation in large group discussion
Cut 3 pieces of paper into 4 sections each. Staple the 12 pieces together at top of paper. Write "My Good Deed Book" on the front page, making it the cover. Sign.	3 pieces of 8x12-inch paper for each student Scissors Markers	Completion of booklet
During the next three days, students will perform one simple act of kindness for a student in the class each day (e.g., sharpen pencils, lend paper or a book, clean up desk, offer to tutor, offer a compliment, play a game together). Students write each day's deed on a separate sheet of paper in their "Good Deed Book." Include date and recipient.	Booklet	Individual students perform a good deed and log it in booklet.
Students perform and log second good deed for another student in the classroom.	Booklet	Individual students perform a good deed and log it in booklet.
Students perform third good deed for another student in the classroom. Review several good deeds performed. How did the these acts make the doer and the recipient feel? Continue deeds.	Booklet	Individual students perform a good deed and log it in booklet.

GOAL: Student recognizes the value of adopting positive character traits.

"Greatness is not found in possessions, power, position, or prestige. It is discovered in goodness, humility, service, and character."
E.C. McKenzie

Display the character trait for the week:
REVIEW OF ALL TRAITS DISCUSSED DURING THE YEAR

Activity	Materials	Evaluation
Discuss quote. How could use of character traits discussed during the year lead to greatness? What are feelings of greatness that a 7th grader would experience?	None	Student participation in group discussion
Have each student design a report card. List each character trait on left side of paper. In center of paper, the student will give him or herself a letter grade (A,B,C,F) for how they have used that trait during the school year.	Paper Pen or pencil	Individual completion of self report card
Using yesterday's self-report card, list examples on the right side of the paper of use of that character trait. Which were easiest to do? Hardest? Cooperative suggesting may help some students.	Yesterday's report card Pen or pencil	Individual completion of self report card
Using yesterday's lists, share results. Were you too hard on yourself with your grades? Is there an area in which you would like to improve?	Yesterday's lists Pen or pencil	Student participation in group discussion
Discuss traits and examples that could be used during the summer vacation time.	Character traits	Student participation in group discussion

GOAL: Student participates responsibly in class citizenship.

"If a child lives with security, he learns to have faith in himself and in those about him.

Dorothy Nolte

Display the character trait for the week:
RESPONSIBILITY

Activity	Materials	Evaluation
Why are rules important? What does citizenship have to do with rules? Brainstorm possible class rules and record them.	Chart paper Markers	Student participation in group activity
Review list of rules. Can they be narrowed? How can the class reach consensus on the rules? Will someone make a motion to accept the rules? Second?	Chart paper Markers List of class rules from yesterday	Student participation in group activity
Have students read the quote. How do rules make you feel secure? Have each student discuss this quote with a partner. Discuss.	List of class rules	Student participation in group activity Individual behavior with partner
What do you do to make yourself feel secure? A small child might have a security blanket. Do you have a routine at bedtime to make yourself feel secure?	Perhaps a "Peanuts" comic strip that could stimulate discussion about Linus' security blanket	Student participation in group activity
Pretend you are an attorney and choose a class rule. How would you defend it?	Chart paper Markers	Student participation in group activity

GOAL: Student participates constructively in making group decisions.

"A chain is as strong as its weakest link."

1868, Concise Oxford Dictionary of Proverbs

Display the character trait for the week:
RESPONSIBILITY

Activity	Materials	Evaluation
Review class rules. Do any changes need to be made? Read the quote. Discuss.	None	Student participation in group activity
Discuss class behavior in cooperative groups? Should any rules be added? Tell them you will be looking for participation. Have each group make a list of traits of a "good citizen."	Chart paper Markers Checklist to record participation	Student participation in large group discussion Individual participation in cooperative groups
Remind students about behavior in cooperative groups. Have each group decide how they can present their traits to the class.	Checklist to record participation	Student participation in cooperative groups
Review class rules. How should students behave during group presentations? Allow part of the groups to present and display their lists.	Checklist of participation, which can be shared following a group's presentation	Student participation in cooperative groups Audience behavior during group presentations
Review rules. Allow additional groups to present. Discuss presentations.	Checklist of participation, which can be shared following a group's presentation	Student participation in cooperative groups Audience behavior during group presentations

GOAL: Student assumes responsibility in routine activities.

"We are here to help one another along life's journey."

William J. Bennett

Display the character trait for the week:
RESPONSIBILITY

Activity	Materials	Evaluation
What is responsibility? Who is responsible? What are you responsible for individually? As a class? Record answers.	Chart paper Markers	Student participation in group activity
Review answers on chart from yesterday. Discuss the quote. Have each student generate an answer in writing to the following: I feel good about myself when I _____. (something you accept responsibility for)	Chart Write statement prompt on board	Student participation in group activity
Remind students about rules for behavior in cooperative groups. Have each group write a "secret" responsibility pact for a task the group will perform during the next two days. After getting consensus, they will write the secret task (e.g., emptying the class trash can prior to leaving class).	Chart Index card for each group Markers Checklist to record responsible behaviors noted in cooperative groups	Student participation in group activity Individual behavior in cooperative groups Secret task turned in from each group
Remind students that they should have started their secret task. Discuss how data can be taken to show results. Have each group discuss and record data on their task on an index card.	Chart Index card for each group Markers Checklist to record responsible behaviors noted in cooperative group	Student participation in large group activity Individual behavior in cooperative groups Card turned in from each group
Conduct a class discussion on what some of the secret tasks might have been. Have each group report and give their data.	Index cards from the two prior group lessons Checklist noting responsible behaviors	Student participation in large group discussion Individual behavior during group presentations

GRADE **8** WEEK **3**

GOAL: Student assumes responsibility in routine activities.

"Man's self-concept is enhanced when he takes responsibility for himself."

William C. Shutz, 1971, Here Comes Everybody

Display the character trait for the week:
RESPONSIBILITY

Activity	Materials	Evaluation
Discuss the quote. How do you show responsibility for yourself? With a partner agree on three things you are responsible for and write on Post-It notes.	Chart paper Post-It notes for pairs Envelope for Post-It notes	Student participation in group discussion Individual behavior in pairs Each pair should turn in three Post-It notes
Review yesterday's quote. Have a volunteer take Post-It and randomly place on chart. Have student volunteers read them to class. Can they be grouped/are there duplicates?	Chart Envelope of Post-It notes Extra Post-Its for headings if some can be grouped in columns	Student participation in group activity
Was homework listed on a Post-It? Why are you responsible for homework? Begin to construct a flow chart for the class as they tell steps in doing homework.	Chart of Post-Its from yesterday Chart paper Markers	Student participation in group activity
Review flow chart from yesterday. Explain that a flow chart shows steps in a process. Have each student do a flow chart of their own homework process.	Chart of homework process Paper Pencils	Student participation in group discussion Individual flowcharts
Ask students why they are responsible for homework. Have volunteers share flow charts.	Chart of homework process Student flow charts	Student participation in group activity

GOAL: ## Student shows responsible behavior in different environments.

"A guilty conscience needs no accuser."

1390, Concise Oxford Dictionary of Proverbs

Display the character trait for the week:
RESPONSIBILITY

Activity	Materials	Evaluation
Discuss the quote. Why does one feel guilty even if no one knows? What are some observable signs of guilt?	None	Student participation in group discussion
Either retell or read excerpts from "The Telltale Heart." What were some observable signs of guilt?	"The Telltale Heart" by Poe	Student participation in group discussion
Brainstorm a list of different environments, such as home, bus, hallways. Group them in categories.	Chart paper Markers	Student participation in group discussion
Review categories of environments. Remind students of behavior in cooperative groups. Tell them you will be observing responsible behavior. Give each group an environment and have them write a slogan for appropriate behavior in it.	Paper Markers Pencils Checklist for responsible behavior	Student behavior during group directions Individual behavior in cooperative groups
Group presentations of slogans beginning with a group that showed responsible behavior.	Group slogans Checklist for responsible behavior	Student behavior during presentations Student participation in presentations

GRADE **8** WEEK **5**

TEACHING CHARACTER IN THE MIDDLE GRADES

77

GOAL: **Student shows respect for authority figures.**

"Have respect for your species. You are a man; do not dishonor mankind."

Jean-Jacques Rousseau

Display the character trait for the week:
RESPECT

Activity	Materials	Evaluation
Read the quote. What is respect? Define it. What are its characteristics? How do you know if you are respected?	Chart paper Markers	Student participation in group activity
Play Aretha Franklin's song, "R-E-S-P-E-C-T" or print some of the lyrics. ("R-E-S-P-E-C-T, find out what it means to me.") Challenge the students to think about what it means to them.	Tape or lyrics from the song	Student participation in group activity
Discuss why it is important to respect authority figures. What would happen if no one did?		Student behavior during class discussion
Have partners volunteer to discuss what they decided respect meant to them.	Song or lyrics from the song Chart from Monday	Student behavior during pairs discussion Student participation in partner activity
What authority figures do you respect? Why? Why would showing respect for authority figures and others show you respect yourself?	Chart Markers	Student participation in group activity

TEACHING CHARACTER IN THE MIDDLE GRADES

Student shows respect for authority figures.

"A man is a worker. If he is not that, he is nothing."

Joseph Conrad

Display the character trait for the week:
RESPECT

Activity	Materials	Evaluation
Discuss the quote. What does it mean. Name workers. How do you show respect for workers?	Chart paper Markers	Student participation in group activity
Review last week's work. How can you show respect for someone who works on your school campus?	Song or lyrics from "Respect" Chart from yesterday and last week	Student participation in group activity
Remind students about behavior in cooperative groups. Tell them you will be watching for respectful behavior. Each group will choose a school worker and decide how they could show respect.	Song and charts from previous respectful activities Pencils and paper for group brainstorms Checklist to tally respectful behavior	Student behavior during group directions Individual behavior in cooperative groups
Review yesterday's project directions. Have groups present their ideas and how they could carry them out. Let them know they can deliver their projects/ messages tomorrow.	Song and charts from previous respectful activities Group ideas	Student behavior during group presentations Behavior as feedback is given to groups
Class will discuss and deliver messages to school authority figures.	Group idea list	Student participation in large group activity Individual participation with their cooperative group

GRADE
8
WEEK
7

GOAL: # Student assumes responsibility for his/her own actions.

"Responsibility is the price of greatness."
Winston Churchill

Display the character trait for the week:
RESPONSIBILITY

Activity	Materials	Evaluation
Discuss the quote. What does it mean? Why does responsibility have a cost?	None	Student participation in group discussion
Remind the students about responsible behavior in cooperative groups. Have each group draw a rule out of the hat. How do you show responsibility for that rule?	Class rules Checklist for responsible student behavior	Student behavior during group direction Student behavior in cooperative groups
Have each group report. Then review the teacher checklist. Did they match?	Class rules Checklist for responsible student behavior	Student behavior during group reports Student behavior during large group discussion
How do you gauge your own behavior? Have each student select a behavior that he/she will monitor in himself/herself for a day.	Class rules	Student behavior during group discussion
Report on your own self-evaluation as the teacher. Have students write anonymous reports and code whether you can read them to the group.	Class rules Student self-evaluation reports with a "may read" code	Student participation in group activity

GOAL: # Student recognizes the need, as a citizen, for rules and laws.

"A law is valuable not because it is law, but because there is right in it."

Henry Ward Beecher

Display the character trait for the week:
RESPONSIBILITY

Activity	Materials	Evaluation
Show the quote. Have students write a sentence about what laws have to do with being a responsible citizen. What does right have to do with responsibility?	Sentence strips Pencils	Student participation in group activity
Have students work with a partner. Have the partners choose a site in the school and write or draw what might happen with no rules.	None Collect student work for discussion at the end of the period	Student participation in group directions,
The Stamp Act was passed by Parliament in 1765. Why was this a problem for the colonists? Why did the colonists institute a boycott? What was "right"? What was their responsibility?	Excerpt from history book about the Stamp Act of 1765	Student participation and behavior in pairs
Remind students about behavior in cooperative groups. Tell them you will be watching for responsibility in the groups. Have each group name a law in history that was challenged.	Paper Pencils Checklist for responsibility	Student participation in group discussion Student behavior during large group directions Individual behavior in cooperative groups
Allow volunteers to present. Have each group brainstorm a school rule that they question. How do you decide if the rule is reasonable if you are responsible?	Paper Pencils Checklist for group responsibility	Student behavior during group report Individual behavior during cooperative group discussion

GOAL: # Student recognizes the need for fair rules and laws.

"Some things have to be believed to be seen."
Ralph Hodgson

Display the character trait for the week:
FAIRNESS

Activity	Materials	Evaluation
Discuss the quote. What would be an example? Have students work in pairs to come up with an example.	None	Student participation in group activity Student participation and behavior with partner
Have the citizens of the past expressed concern about the fairness of laws? Why did American colonists oppose British policies? Have students work in pairs to make up a "quote" from the past.	Paper Pencils and pens Markers Sentence strips	Student behavior during large group directions Student participation and behavior with partner
Read quotes and have students guess who said it and what the opposition was.	Quotes	Student participation in group activity
How do we find out about issues in our government? What are some issues of concern? How does fairness come into view?	Newspapers for examples	Student participation in group activity
Have student volunteers share their article topics or headlines. Do any have "to be believed to be seen"? Is the policy fair?	Newspapers for examples Student topics and headlines	Student participation in group activity

TEACHING CHARACTER IN THE MIDDLE GRADES

GOAL: # Student analyzes classroom problems and comes up with solutions.

"Learn not to sweat the small stuff."

Dr. Kenneth Greenspan

Display the character trait for the week:
GOOD JUDGMENT

Activity	Materials	Evaluation
Under the term Good Judgment, make columns for "small stuff" and "major stuff." Read the quote and have the class brainstorm for items to list.	Chart paper Markers	Student participation in group activity
Have students work with a partner. Have the pairs write a school problem that they have noticed (e.g., noise in the halls, trash in the public areas). Collect paper from each pair at the end of the period.	Paper Pencils	Student participation in group directions Student behavior in pairs
Share the pairs' school scenarios. Is it "big stuff" or "small stuff"?	Partnership papers from previous day Chart Markers	Student participation in group discussion Student participation in group presentation
Review chart. Remind students about behavior in cooperative groups. Have groups select a different school problem scenario and discuss possible solutions. Tell them you will be looking for good judgment.	Cards Chart Checklist to record good judgment	Student participation in group activity Student participation in cooperative groups
Start by reporting signs of good judgment. Allow group volunteers to present the problem and possible solution. Have class react. Is that a viable solution?	Cards Checklist Chart to record class solutions	Student participation in large group activity Student participation in group presentation

GOAL: Student analyzes classroom problems and comes up with solutions.

"We must hang together or assuredly we shall hang separately."
Benjamin Franklin

Display the character trait for the week:
GOOD JUDGMENT

Activity	Materials	Evaluation
Review the class problems and possible solutions from last week. Discuss the quote. How does it relate?	Cards from last week Chart of problems and possible solutions	Student participation in group discussion
How do problems in government/ business get addressed? Brainstorm.	Chart paper Markers	Student participation in group discussion
Use list from yesterday. Can we use any of these methods to come up with a plan to address our class problems? Select one problem and apply the method. Can the class agree to try it until Friday?	Brainstorm list Problem/solution chart	Student behavior during reports Individual participation in reports
Review discussion from yesterday. Write the problem and solution plan. Does everyone agree?	Problem/solution chart Chart paper Markers	Student behavior during group directions Individual participation in activity
Discuss problem and new plan. Have each student write a brief self-evaluation of how the new plan has been working since Wednesday.	Copy of plan Paper Pencils	Student behavior during presentations Individual participation in activity

GOAL: Student respects likenesses and differences in people.

"People do not seem to realize that their opinion of the world is also a confession of character."

Ralph Waldo Emerson

Display the character trait for the week:
RESPECT

Activity	Materials	Evaluation
Discuss the quote. How do you react to the opinions of others? How do you show respect for the opinions of others? What does that have to do with character?	None	Student participation in group activity
Read excerpts or give a synopsis of "Flowers for Algernon" by Daniel Keyes. What opinion did others have of Charlie? Was he respected? Did the viewpoint change?	"Flowers for Algernon" by Daniel Keyes	Student participation in group discussion
Remind students about behavior in cooperative groups. Have each group select a topic or situation and draw a cartoon to depict possible reactions from others. Tell them you will be looking for images of respect.	Paper Pencils Cards with topics such as: You became a genius overnight, You won the lottery, You failed a major test, You have to move away, Your clothes were all burned in a fire, etc. Checklist for respect	Student participation in group directions Individual participation in cooperative groups
Review yesterday's assignment. Remind students about behavior in cooperative groups and that you will be looking for respect. Have groups complete their cartoons.	Same as previous day	Student participation in large group directions Individual participation in cooperative groups
Group presentations of cartoons. Is respect fleeting depending on the situation? Discuss.	Group cartoons	Student behavior during group presentations Individual participation in group presentations

GOAL: **Student recognizes examples of community service.**

"Charity begins at home"

1383, Concise Oxford Dictionary of Proverbs

Display the character trait for the week:
RESPONSIBILITY

Activity	Materials	Evaluation
Discuss the quote. What is charity? Is it good? Why are we responsible? What charitable services are done at home? Is there another meaning for "home"?	None	Student participation in group discussion
What types of community service are provided at school? Brainstorm. Is that like "charity begins at home"? How does a student become involved in school/ community services? Ask who's involved in each group—graph.	Chart Markers Paper for graph	Student participation in group discussion
Remind students about behavior in cooperative groups. Have each group name something their group could do for the school between now and Friday. Tell them you will be observing responsibility.	Graph Checklist to record respon- sible behavior	Student behavior during group directions Student behavior in cooperative groups
Have each group report on their proposed activity. Have they started it? Will they be ready to report by tomorrow?	Checklist of responsible behavior	Student participation in group discussion
Have each group report on their activity and any response they received. Will you always know that community service is appreciated?	Checklist of responsible behavior	Student participation in group discussion Student participation in group reports

TEACHING CHARACTER IN THE MIDDLE GRADES

GOAL: Student distinguishes between wants and needs.

"You can tell the ideals of a nation by its advertisements."

Norman Douglas

Display the character trait for the week:
SELF-DISCIPLINE

Activity	Materials	Evaluation
Discuss the quote. Brainstorm examples. Ask students to bring in ads tomorrow.	Chart paper Markers Sample ads from magazines	Student participation in group discussion
Put up a column for Wants and one for Needs. As students volunteer their ads, decide as a group where the product goes.	Chart paper Markers Music in the background could be "You Can't Always Get What You Want" (Rolling Stones)	Student participation in group activity
Remind students about behavior in cooperative groups. What is the purpose of advertising? Have each group choose an ad. Does it advertise a want or need? Whom are they advertising to? Record examples of self-discipline in groups.	Paper, pencils Ads Checklist to record self-discipline	Student behavior during group directions Individual behavior in cooperative groups
Have groups show their ads and explain what the advertiser was trying to get you to do. How effective were they—do you want to go out and buy it? Were they wants or needs? How does self-discipline relate to wants and needs? Have students bring in ads for items they like, want, or need.	Group ads from the past Checklist of examples of self-discipline	Student participation in large group discussio Individual participation in group presentation
As students volunteer to show their ads, decide how they reflect the values of our nation. Is that how we want to be viewed?	Ads from previous lessons Checklist of examples of self-discipline	Student participation in group discussion

GOAL: Student predicts the consequences of responsible and irresponsible actions.

"Where there's life, there's hope."
Aesop

Display the character trait for the week:
RESPONSIBILITY

Activity	Materials	Evaluation
Have you made mistakes? Errors in judgment? How did you deal with those? Discuss the quote. Have each student write something he wishes he had not done. Then as a group, all tear them up simultaneously to show symbolically that you can go forward from a mistake.	Paper Pencils	Student participation in group activity
Write Responsible–Irresponsible on the board. Have student pairs generate a list for each. Take up lists.	Chart Markers	Student behavior during group directions Student participation in paired activity
Remind students about behavior in cooperative groups. Give each group a slip of paper with an irresponsible action on it. The group will generate possible consequences. Tell them you will be observing responsible behavior.	Student lists cut apart into irresponsible actions Checklist for responsible behaviors Paper Pencils	Student behavior during group activity Individual behavior and participation in cooperative groups
Remind students about behavior in cooperative groups. Have groups develop a role play for the irresponsible action and one of their possible consequences from the previous day.	Group products from previous day Checklist for responsible behaviors	Student behavior during group activity Individual behavior and participation in cooperative groups
Read excerpts from checklist of responsible behaviors. What are the consequences of responsible behavior? Have groups perform role plays.	Group products from Wednesday and role-play ideas Checklist of responsible behavior	Student participation in group activity Individual participation in role plays

TEACHING CHARACTER IN THE MIDDLE GRADES

GOAL: # Student explains the need to apply rules fairly.

"Winning is not everything. It's the only thing."
Vince Lombardi

Display the character trait for the week:
FAIRNESS

Activity	Materials	Evaluation
Vince Lombardi was a coach. Do you think that someone who plays only to win would always be a fair player? What happens to someone like that who loses? How are fairness and sportsmanship related?	None	Student participation in group activity
Why is it necessary to apply rules fairly? Brainstorm a list of sports and games. Have student pairs choose a game and write a list of the rules.	Chart paper Marker	Student participation in group discussion Individual participation in paired activity
Divide the class into teams. Play a game like Outburst. Give team the name of a game and they have one minute to yell out all the rules. Team gets a point for each that matches the pair list from previous day. Tell students to bring in cutouts of sports pictures.	Chart for score Marker Pair game rules from yesterday	Student participation in group game
Remind students about behavior in cooperative groups. Tell them you will look for fair behavior. Have groups come up with a sports motto that emphasizes fairness rather than just winning. They can use their cutouts for the mottoes.	Paper Markers Cutouts of sports pictures	Student behavior during group directions Individual behavior during cooperative group activity
Have groups volunteer to show and tell about their mottoes.	Group mottoes	Student participation in group discussion Individual participation in group presentations

GOAL: **Student establishes rapport with his/her peer group.**

"It is easy to flatter; it is harder to praise."
Jean Paul Richter

Display the character trait for the week:
RESPECT

Activity	Materials	Evaluation
Discuss the quote. Have partners practice flattery and praise with a partner. Discuss again. What is the difference?	None	Student participation in group activity
Why is praise more difficult? Have students write a description of their best friend and why they like them.	Paper Pencils Student descriptions	Student participation in group discussion Individual participation in writing activity
Have students look at the description of their friend. Have students write praise statements they could say to their friend.	Paper Pencils	Student participation in writing activity
How does praise make you feel? Make a list of your inner feelings when you receive praise. Are they different in different situations?	Paper Pencils	Student participation in group activity
Have volunteers give examples from the previous day. Why would praise make you feel uncomfortable, nervous, excited, etc.	Collect student work Student examples	Student behavior during group discussion

TEACHING CHARACTER IN THE MIDDLE GRADES

GOAL: Student respects his/her own personal possessions.

"It is an immutable law of kite flying that the one holding the string is in charge."

Donald G. Smith

Display the character trait for the week:
RESPECT

Activity	Materials	Evaluation
Have students close their eyes and visualize the quote as you read it. What did they see? Discuss the quote.	None	Student participation in group discussion
How do you show respect for personal possessions? Brainstorm possessions that one has for a long period of time. What respect is required? Make list.	Chart paper Markers	Student participation in group discussion
Show chart to remind them of yesterday's discussion. Have student pairs talk about their favorite personal possession and write each on a Post-It note.	Chart Post-It notes	Student participation in pairs activity
Take Post-It notes and have class think of different ways to group them.	Chart Post-It notes	Student participation in group activity
Review Post-Its from yesterday. Do those possessions require care and respect? Have students in pairs take turns pretending to be the other's favorite possession. What would the possession say about its care and respect? Allow volunteers to share.	Chart Post-It notes	Student behavior during pairs activity Student behavior as volunteers share

GRADE
8
WEEK
19

GOAL: Student respects the personal possessions of others.

"There is no right way to do the wrong thing."
Anonymous

Display the character trait for the week:
RESPECT

Activity	Materials	Evaluation
Discuss the quote. Have student volunteers retell the story of Goldilocks and the Three Bears as a modern-day story. How would Goldilocks justify her actions?	None.	Student participation in group activity
Retell or have students retell "Petty Larceny" by Jessica Saiki. Why is stealing wrong? Why does taking a personal possession make one feel guilty?	"Petty Larceny" by Jessica Saiki (Literature and Language—if unavailable, relate back to Goldilocks)	Student participation in group discussion
How many descriptive words can you think of that would describe respect for the possessions of others? Have student pairs write descriptive words on Post-It notes.	Paper Pencils Post-It notes	Student behavior during group directions Individual behavior during pairs activity
As you read descriptive words, place them on a chart. Have student volunteers choose words, read them and name a possession it could apply to.	Post-It notes Chart paper	Student participation in group activity
Select a few personal possessions from yesterday and have the class come up with Care Instructions. When you borrow something should the owner remind you of care instructions?	Chart paper Markers	Student participation in group activity

GOAL: Student exhibits self-discipline.

"Keep company with those who may make you better."

English Proverb

Display the character trait for the week:
SELF-DISCIPLINE

Activity	Materials	Evaluation
Discuss the quote. How can the company you keep make you better? Brainstorm. Is the opposite true?	None	Student participation in group discussion
How can you show self-control about the company you keep? What are ways to tactfully say "no"? Have partners discuss and see if any will volunteer their suggestions.	None	Student behavior during group directions Individual behavior during pairs activity Student behavior as individuals share
What are some situations when you may have to exercise self-discipline? Brainstorm and list.	Chart paper Markers	Student behavior during group discussion
Present the situations from the chart. As a volunteer, "Where do you stand?" Have student pretend that the center of the room is no opinion, right is yes, left is no. As you state a topic, students will move. Ask if they felt peer pressure.	List from yesterday	Student participation in group activity
Have students pick a topic and write themselves a note about how they plan to exercise self-discipline.	Paper Pencils	Student participation in group activity

GRADE
8
WEEK
21

GOAL: Student is a good listener.

"If a man be gracious, and courteous to strangers, it shows he is a citizen of the world."

Francis Bacon

Display the character trait for the week:
RESPECT

GRADE
8
WEEK
22

Activity	Materials	Evaluation
Have students read the quote and rethink it in their own words as it relates to kindness.	None	Student participation in group discussion
Describe a good listener. Why is it important to be a good listener? Brainstorm various careers. Is listening part of the job description? Have students observe good listening and be prepared to report back.	Chart paper Markers	Student participation in group discussion
As a class, come up with a few steps to good listening based on their observation such: sit quietly, keep eyes on the speaker, reflective statements, summarizing, etc.	Chart paper Markers	Student participation in group discussion
Give the students interview questions. Have them practice interviewing a partner. Have a rating scale for the partner to rate them on as a listener. Challenge them to interview one of the adults at school and report back. (You could have the adult rate the student as an interviewer.)	List of five interview questions (e.g. Where are you from? What are your hobbies? What is the biggest concern in America today?) Rating scale from 1-5 on interviewer: uses eye contact, listens attentively, gives positive feedback, etc.	Student behavior during group directions Individual behavior in pairs activity
Have students discuss their reactions as interviewer and to their ratings as a good interviewer. Was listening important? Why?	Interview questions and ratings	Student behavior during group activity

94

TEACHING CHARACTER IN THE MIDDLE GRADES

GOAL: # Student works independently.

"No one knows what he can do until he tries."

Publius Syrius

Display the character trait for the week:
RESPONSIBILITY

Activity	Materials	Evaluation
Discuss the quote. Have you ever done something well on your own and then been surprised by your success? Have student pairs discuss this. What helped you achieve that surprising goal?	None	Student participation in large group discussion Individual behavior in pairs activity
What are some strategies for working independently? Discuss. Have students commit to trying a strategy and reporting on it by Friday. Organizational strategies are good for fostering independent work.	Chart Marker	Student participation in group discussion
Remind students that they should keep on trying the study strategy they will report upon. Brainstorm different areas of school life where one must show responsibility.	Chart Marker	Student participation in group discussion
Remind students about behavior in cooperative groups. Have each group select an area of school life to illustrate and write a Responsibility Statement for behavior in that area. Tell them you will be observing responsibility.	Paper Colored pencils, markers, pencils Chart with list of areas of school life Checklist for responsible behavior	Student behavior during group directions Individual participation in cooperative groups
Have student volunteers report on their study strategy. Report to them on responsible behavior. Allow groups to present their illustrations for discussion and display.	Chart Tape Checklist of responsible behavior	Student participation in group discussion Individual participation in cooperative group presentation

GRADE
8
WEEK
23

GOAL: Student accepts constructive criticism.

"It is better to know some of the questions than all of the answers."

Anonymous saying

Display the character trait for the week:
PERSEVERANCE

Activity	Materials	Evaluation
Discuss the quote. What is constructive criticism? Why is it important? Have a volunteer draw a card, read the career choice, and have the class generate why constructive criticism would be critical to their success.	Cards with careers written on them	Student participation in group activity
Explain that groups will try new activities with an expert to develop a positive attitude about constructive criticism. Have them begin to think of an activity they could teach.	Chart paper Markers	Student participation in group activity
Have class members volunteer for activities they could teach (e.g., basketball pass, tennis serve, backstroke). Make list and have the class vote on the ones they most want to try.	Materials for groups to use, if necessary Checklist for perseverance	Student behavior during group directions Individual behavior in cooperative groups
Remind students about behavior in cooperative groups. Have an "expert" for each group and allow students to choose a group to join. "Experts" will give constructive criticism as students attempt activity. You will observe perseverance.	Same as previous day	Student behavior during group directions Individual behavior in cooperative groups
Do same activity as Wednesday, but allow students to switch groups. Conduct discussion on perseverance in the groups and how students accept constructive criticism.	Checklist on perseverance	Student participation in group discussion

GOAL: Student interacts appropriately with his/her peer group.

"Are we having fun yet?"
Zippy the Pinhead comic strip, 1979

Display the character trait for the week:
FAIRNESS

Activity	Materials	Evaluation
Have students close their eyes as you read the quote. When they open their eyes, have them share their favorite sports/games with a partner.	None	Student participation in large group discussion individual participation in pairs activity
Remind students about behavior in cooperative groups. Have each group generate a set of Bingo cards on their favorite sports and sports stars. Tell them you will observe fairness.	Paper for Bingo cards Cards for words Rulers Pencils, markers Checklist for fairness	Student behavior during group directions Individual behavior in cooperative groups
Remind students about behavior in cooperative groups. Groups will continue work on their Bingo cards. If they finish, they should begin a game.	Paper for Bingo cards Cards for words Rulers Pencils Checklist for fairness	Student behavior during group directions Individual behavior in cooperative groups
Remind students about behavior in cooperative groups and fairness with game rules. Groups will play Sports Bingo. Teacher will observe fairness.	Group Sports Bingo materials (e.g. beans for markers) Checklist for fairness	Student behavior during group directions Individual behavior in cooperative groups
Share your observations on fairness. Conduct discussion on how the group Sports Bingo went. How do you feel when others don't exhibit fair play?	Checklist for fairness	Student participation in group discussion

GRADE
8
WEEK
25

GOAL: **Student talks appropriately with his/her peer group.**

"Things that are done, it is needless to speak about…things that are past, it is needless to blame."
Confucius.

Display the character trait for the week:
RESPECT

Activity	Materials	Evaluation
Discuss the quote. Have students think of something from history that the quote could go with. Brainstorm.	None	Student participation in group discussion
The goal is for students to talk appropriately with their peer group. How does that vary in different environments? Think of different environments within the school or neighborhood. How would the language be different? Brainstorm.	Chart paper Markers	Student participation in group discussion
Have students describe different types of graphic organizers. Select a graphic organizer and describe the classroom with regard to school rules and procedures and appropriate language.	Chart paper Markers Paper Pencils	Student participation in group discussion
Remind students about behavior in cooperative groups. Allow groups to select an environment, choose a graphic organizer and describe the appropriate language (no profanity allowed). Tell them you will observe respect as they work.	Checklist for respect	Student behavior during group directions Individual behavior in cooperative groups
Review the quote. Ask for groups to volunteer to report. How does appropriate language show respect?	Group graphic organizers	Student participation in group discussion

GOAL: ## Student can keep a secret.

"Every cause produces more than one effect."

Essays on Education, 1861

Display the character trait for the week:
RESPONSIBILITY

Activity	Materials	Evaluation
Discuss the quote. How can telling someone's secret produce more than one effect? Have you ever had a secret that was told? How did you feel? Have pairs discuss.	None	Student participation in group discussion Individual participation in pairs activity
Why would you have to decide if telling a secret was your responsibility? Have pairs come up with a time that a secret must be told. Share.	None	Student participation in group discussion Individual participation in pairs activity
Remind students about behavior in cooperative groups. Have each group start a story, illustration or cartoon that involves keeping a secret but not finish it. Tell them you will observe responsibility.	Paper Colored pencils or markers Checklist for responsible behavior Group story/picture starters	Student behavior during group directions Individual behavior in cooperative group
Remind students about behavior in cooperative groups. Give each group a story or picture starter generated by another group and they will complete it. Tell them you will observe responsibility.	Paper Colored pencils or markers Checklist for responsible behavior	Student behavior during group directions Individual behavior in cooperative group
Talk about keeping a secret versus having responsibility. Have groups share their stories and the class should evaluate their choices.	Group completed stories/pictures Checklist of responsible behavior	Student participation in group discussion Individual participation in group presentations

GRADE 8
WEEK 27

GOAL: Student expresses affection appropriately.

"Love comforteth like sunshine after rain."
Shakespeare

Display the character trait for the week:
GOOD JUDGMENT

Activity	Materials	Evaluation
Discuss the quote. Have students discuss different types of love. Note them on chart. What are appropriate expressions of each? How do you know?	Chart paper Marker	Student participation in group discussion
Review different types of love from previous day. Have student pairs choose one and generate a sentence scenario. Allow them to share with class.	Chart Paper Pencils	Student participation in group review Individual participation in pairs activity
Remind students about behavior in cooperative groups. Have each group choose a sentence scenario and develop a 1-minute "take a stand" speech on whether or not it is socially appropriate. Tell students you will observe good judgment.	Chart Paper Pencils Sentence scenarios Checklist on good judgment	Student behavior during group directions Individual behavior in cooperative groups
Remind students about behavior in cooperative groups. Have groups determine who their "Take a Stand on the Soapbox" presenter will be for a 1-minute speech.	Speeches Checklist on good judgment	Student behavior during group directions Individual behavior in cooperative groups
Have presenters give their 1-minute speeches. Critique with constructive criticism. Did their stand demonstrate good judgment?	Speeches Timer Something to represent a "soapbox" to stand on Checklist on good judgment	Student participation in group activity Individual participation in soapbox speeches

GOAL: **Student understands the difference between right and wrong.**

"I leave this rule for others when I'm dead:
Be always sure you're right—then go ahead."

David Crockett (1786-1836)

Display the character trait for the week:
COURAGE

Activity	Materials	Evaluation
Discuss the quote. What does it mean? How can you be sure you're right? If you could write a rule for others to follow, what would it be?	None	Student participation in group activity
Why does it take courage to stand up for your own convictions? Have student pairs think of famous people who stood up for their convictions.	Paper Pencils	Student participation in group discussion Individual participation in pairs activity
Have groups select a famous person from history who stood up for his/her convictions and write a statement to depict their viewpoint. Was the person right? Ask students to make up a quote that person might have said.	Paper Colored pencils, markers	Student behavior during group directions Individual behavior in cooperative groups
Remind students about behavior in cooperative groups. Allow groups to take time to complete their projects.	Paper Colored pencils, markers	Student behavior during group directions Individual behavior in cooperative groups
Let groups volunteer to present their courageous quotes. Did this person's stand for right have an impact on history?	Group projects	Student participation in group activity Individual participation in cooperative groups

Student understands the consequences of his/her actions.

"Those who'll play with cats must expect to be scratched."

Miguel de Cervantes

Display the character trait for the week:
RESPONSIBILITY

Activity	Materials	Evaluation
Discuss the quote. Are there times when the consequences of your actions affect more than you? Are the results always positive or negative? Discuss.	None	Student participation in group discussion
"In a national survey, of more than 6,000 college freshmen and sophomores, 76% admitted to cheating." What are the possible consequences? Are there consequences if no one ever catches you? Who is responsible? Why?	Chart paper Markers (Statistic cited by Thomas Lickona, Educating for Character (1991)	Student participation in group discussion
What are some actions you should stop and think about that might produce negative consequences? Have student pairs generate a list.	Paper Pencils	Student participation in group discussion Individual participation in pairs activity
Divide the room into three territories—negative, neutral, positive. As you read an action have students move to the area which depicts the type consequence.	Pairs lists from yesterday	Student participation in group activity
What is a geometric progression? Have the cooperative groups choose a negative consequence from the previous day and write the progression of all the individuals the wrong choice could impact.	Paper Pencils Tell them the sequence beginning "For want of a nail, the horseshoe was lost, for want of a horseshoe, the horse was lost..."	Student participation in group activity

GOAL: Student can handle competition.

"You know how to win a victory, Hannibal, but not how to use it."

Maharbal Barca the Carthaginian, 210 B.C.

Display the character trait for the week:
FAIRNESS

Activity	Materials	Evaluation
Discuss the quote. How does one "use" a victory? Discuss graciousness in winning. Name and discuss gracious winners in sports.	None	Student participation in group discussion
Review the quote. Have you ever seen someone be a poor loser? How about an offensive winner? What were the signs? What strategies can you use when you lose? Have student pairs discuss and share their views.	None	Student participation in group discussionI Individual participation in pairs activity
Decide to hold a class competition. Brainstorm quick competitions that the class might do: spelling bee, Bingo, War, etc. Vote and determine who will provide materials for the groups.	Chart paper Markers	Student participation in class discussion
Begin competition in groups and narrow by elimination. Conduct as many trials as time permits. Tell students you will observe fairness.	Competition materials Timer Checklist for fairness	Student behavior during group directions Individual behavior in cooperative groups
Discuss fairness. Were winners and losers gracious? Discuss and hold mock awards ceremony.	Paper ribbons for Winners and Losers Checklist for fairness	Student participation in group activity

GRADE
8
WEEK
31

GOAL: Student has an appropriate sense of humor.

"Humor clears the head and heals the soul."
Nancy Henley

Display the character trait for the week:
JOYFULNESS

Activity	Materials	Evaluation
Discuss the quote. How does it feel when you laugh? Why is it important to be joyful? Explain what "appropriate humor" is. Challenge the students to find something appropriately humorous to share with the group.	None	Student participation in group discussion
Share something humorous with the class such as a Shel Silverstein poem or Shel Silverstein on tape. Discuss. Remind students to search for something humorous for Friday.	Shel Silverstein, *A Light in the Attic, Where the Side-walk Ends* (these can be found on audiotape also)	Student participation in group discussion
Share a humorous anecdote about yourself. Remind students about behavior in cooperative groups. Have groups share humorous stories about themselves. Were they appropriate?	Checklist for appropriate humor	Student behavior during group discussion Individual participation in cooperative groups
Share a favorite cartoon with the class. Why is it funny? Have student pairs share cartoons.	Cartoons from the local newspaper	Student behavior during group directions Individual behavior in pairs activity
Have individuals share appropriately humorous jokes or stories. Discuss. How has this week of joyfulness made you feel? Why does the word "appropriate" have to accompany "humor"?	None	Student participation in group activity

TEACHING CHARACTER IN THE MIDDLE GRADES

GOAL: Student can adapt to change.

"We are the world, we are the children,
We are the ones to make a better day."
"We are the world."

Lionel Richie

Display the character trait for the week:
COURAGE

Activity	Materials	Evaluation
Discuss the quote. Why does it take courage to face change? What are times in your life when there was a lot of change? What does it mean to "embrace change"? Ask students to interview a grandparent or senior citizen to record changes they have observed and report on Friday.	None	Student participation in group discussion
Remind students about Friday reports. Review the concept that life brings about constant change. Have student pairs construct personal timelines, noting big changes. Allow them to share. Tell them to bring their social studies books tomorrow.	Paper Pencils	Student behavior during group activity Individual behavior in pairs activity
Remind students about behavior in cooperative groups. Have each group select a time period in history and construct a timeline of the "change agents" present.	Paper Colored pencils	Student behavior during group activity Individual behavior in cooperative groups
Read an excerpt from *The Diary of Anne Frank*. How did she have to face change? Was courage involved? How?	*The Diary of Anne Frank*	Student participation in group discussion
Have student volunteers present what they discovered during their interviews. Discuss. Did the interviewees have to adapt to change?	None	Student participation in group activity

GOAL: Student controls his/her anger.

"To rule one's anger is well; to prevent it is still better."
Tyron Edwards

Display the character trait for the week:
SELF-DISCIPLINE

Activity	Materials	Evaluation
Discuss the quote. What is the difference between the first part and the second part? What are some strategies for the first? The second?	Chart paper Markers	Student participation in group discussion
Review strategies for controlling one's anger. Tell students to observe this week and cite any examples they see by Friday. Have student pairs practice and discuss the strategies of their choice.	Chart Markers	Student behavior during group directions Individual participation in pairs activity
Review strategies for preventing anger. Remind students to observe the behavior of others. Have student pairs discuss the control and prevention strategies of their choice.	Chart from Monday	Student behavior during group directions Individual participation in pairs activity
Read some excerpts from *The Diary of Anne Frank* or *Harriet Tubman: Conductor on the Underground Railroad*. Why do scenes from the Holocaust or slavery still inspire anger? Have student pairs discuss things that make them angry.	The Diary of Anne Frank Harriet Tubman: Conductor on the Underground Railroad, by Ann Petry, or other related selections	Student behavior during group activity Individual participation in pairs activity
Review the quote and strategies for controlling and preventing anger. Have students report on their observations. Discuss.	Chart from Monday	Student participation in group discussion

GOAL: Student communicates his/her needs appropriately.

"Half the truth is often a great lie."

Benjamin Franklin

Display the character trait for the week:
HONESTY

Activity	Materials	Evaluation
Discuss the quote. What is "half the truth"? Do you ever stretch the truth? What is a white lie? Are they ever justified?	None	Student participation in group discussion
Review the quote. Brainstorm times when it is difficult to tell the truth. Have student pairs list additional examples and share.	Chart paper Markers	Student behavior during group directions Individual participation in pairs activity
Use the pairs' lists to make a large class list. Have student pairs choose one example and write an appropriate dialogue to resolve the issue.	Chart paper Markers Pairs' lists Pencils Paper	Student behavior during group discussion Individual participation in pairs activity
Review yesterday's activity. Have the same student pairs practice the dialogue they wrote and read both parts. Be sure that they include an appropriate resolution with honesty. Have one of the pairs agree to present their example tomorrow.	Chart Markers Pairs' lists and dialogues	Student behavior during group discussion Individual participation in pairs activity
Remind students how to render constructive criticism. Remind them that the goal is appropriate and honest communication. Have students present and class critique. How does being honest help you get your needs met?	Chart Pairs' lists and dialogues	Student participation in group activity

GOAL: Student respects the environment.

"Heaven is under our feet as well as over our heads"

Henry David Thoreau (1817-1862)

Display the character trait for the week:
RESPECT

Activity	Materials	Evaluation
Have students close their eyes as you read the quote. After they open their eyes, have them illustrate what the quote means to them.	Paper Colored Pencils	Student participation in group activity
Read excerpts to the class from *The Maine Woods* or *On Walden Pond* or any reading about the beauty in nature. What are things we should do to show respect for the environment?	*The Maine Woods*, *On Walden Pond* by Henry David Thoreau (or other related reading) Chart paper Markers	Student participation in group activity
Have students name various school environments. What are things we do at school to show respect for the environment? What are things we could do? Brainstorm.	Chart paper Markers	Student participation in group discussion
Remind students about behavior in cooperative groups. Have each group choose a way to express their respect for the environment (e.g., story, poem, illustration, song). Tell them you will observe respect.	Paper Pencils Markers colored pencils Checklist for respect	Student behavior during group directions Individual behavior in cooperative groups
Reread the quote. Have groups present their own treatise on "Respect for the Environment."	Group presentations	Student participation in group discussion Individual participation in cooperative groups

Index of Lessons
by Character Trait

Bibliography

Africa, Asia, and Pacific Realm. Raleigh, NC: Humanities Extension/Publications Program, North Carolina State University, 1998.

Bartlett, John and Justin Kaplan. *Bartlett's Familiar Quotations*. Boston: Little, Brown and Company, 1992.

Bell, Dr. John L., Jr. and Dr. Jeffrey J. Crow. *North Carolina: The History of an American State*. Montgomery, Ala.: Clairmont Press, 1998.

Berman, Louis A. *Proverb Wit & Wisdom*. New York: The Berkley Publishing Co., 1997.

Broome, Sadie Allran and Nancy Henley. *Teaching Character: It's Elementary*. Chapel Hill, N.C.: Character Development Publishing, 2000.

Canfield, Jack and Harold C. Wells. *100 Ways to Enhance Self-Concept in the Classroom*. Englewood, N.J.: Prentice-Hall, 1976.

Dotson, Anne C. and Karen D. Dodson. *Teaching Character: Teacher's Idea Book*. Chapel Hill, N.C.: Character Development Group, 1997.

Lickona, Thomas. E*ducating for Character*. New York.: Bantam Books, 1991.

Literature and Language. Evanston, Ill.: McDougal Littell, Inc. A Houghton Mifflin Company, 1994.

McKenzie, E. C. *14,000 Quips & Quotes*. New York: Crown Publishers, Inc., 1984.

Silverstein, Shel. *A Light in the Attic*. New York: Harper & Row, 1981.

_____. *Where the Sidewalk Ends*. New York: Harper & Row, 1981.

Simpson, John A., ed. *Concise Oxford Dictionary of Proverbs*. New York: Oxford University Press, 1982.

Stevenson, Burton. *The Home Book of Proverbs, Maxims, and Familiar Phrases*. New York: MacMillan, 1948.

Tessler, Diane Jane. *Drugs, Kids, and Schools*. Glenview, Ill.: Scott, Foresman and Company, 1980.

Vincent, Philip Fitch. *Developing Character in Students: A Primer for Teachers, Parents & Communities*. Chapel Hill, N.C.: Character Development Group, 1997.

Webster's 21st Century Book of Quotations. Nashville, Tenn.: Thomas Nelson Publishers, 1992.

About the Authors

Sadie Allran Broome is an Instructional Specialist with the Gaston County Schools in Gastonia, North Carolina. Prior to her position as Instructional Specialist, she taught exceptional children for eighteen years in the area of Behaviorally Emotionally Handicapped. She was a Gaston County Teacher of the Year. Sadie and her co-author were joint recipients of a Christa McAuliffe Fellowship, which featured a model program for the Behaviorally Emotionally Handicapped entitled "The Magic Kids." A significant part of the Magic Kid program involved daily class meetings with a focus on development of social skills and character traits.

Ms. Broome has co-authored an article with Dr. Richard White in Teaching Exceptional Children entitled "The Many Uses of Videotape in Classrooms Serving Youth with Behavioral Disorders." She has also published an article in Beyond Behavior entitled "Magic in the Classroom." She and Nancy W. Henley co-authored *Teaching Character...It's Elementary*.

Nancy W. Henley has worked as a teacher of behaviorally and emotionally handicapped students for 21 years. She has spent most of her career teaching in self contained BEH classes in public elementary schools. During seven of those years, she taught in partnership with co-author Sadie Allran Broome. Together, they have also taught in-service classes for teachers, presented at local and national conferences, and written successful grant projects, including the prestigious Christa McAuliffe Fellowship awarded by the U.S. Department of Education.

Ms. Henley is now in her third year of teaching at Court Drive School, an intensive day treatment program for students with behavior disorders and psychiatric diagnoses in grades K-12. The school operates under the dual auspices of Gaston County Schools and the Gaston/Lincoln/Cleveland Mental Health Authority. Teaching social skills and important character traits is always critical with these students. Deficiencies in this area make it difficult for most BEH students to get their needs met, and is a frequent antecedent to frustration and explosive behavior. In her years in the public schools, Ms. Henley has observed non-disabled students in various settings and found that many of them could also benefit from systematic character education. She is committed to the belief that self esteem is built through competence, not compliments. "Praise is important," she says, "but if you want to help a kid feel successful and valuable, teach him how to do something."

She and Sadie Allran Broome co-authored *Teaching Character...It's Elementary*.

Elizabeth Mordaszewski has been a teacher for 29 years. She began teaching English to grades 10, 11, and 12 at Pittsfield High School, in her hometown of Pittsfield, Mass. She also taught Research and Individualized Communication Skills, and she supervised students working on the school newspaper. She made presentations at local, state, and national conventions for the Council of Teachers of English. When she married, she followed her husband's family to Gastonia, N.C., where she spent 16 years as a Language Arts teacher of the behaviorally and emotionally handicapped students in grades 3-12 at Court Drive School, a ground-breaking intensive day treatment program.

In 1996, Ms. Mordaszewski became the Behavioral Management Specialist for Gaston County Schools. She has enjoyed the job immensely, taking her as it does into all 52 schools in Gaston County and allowing her to help teachers and administrators with the most challenging behaviors of students. She consults with teachers, parents and local agencies to coordinate the referral for services and tries to reach out to provide any assistance possible for children and teachers. She is responsible for the training of 30 Behavior Lab Specialists in the use of social skills and other techniques to assist them in the management of students with in-school suspension. She oversees Student Management Services in each school, the group that helps deal with intervention strategies for referred students, and students who are disabled under Section 504. She presents staff development to teachers and parents on classroom management and intervention strategies. For many years she tutored students in the Juvenile Justice System to increase their self-esteem and success in school. This is her first publication.

Create an Activity

GOAL:

Activity	Materials	Evaluation

Create an Activity

GOAL:

Activity	Materials	Evaluation

Create an Activity

GOAL:

Activity	Materials	Evaluation

Create an Activity

GOAL:

Activity	Materials	Evaluation

Create an Activity

GOAL:

Activity	Materials	Evaluation

TEACHING CHARACTER IN THE MIDDLE GRADES

Create an Activity

GOAL:

Activity	Materials	Evaluation

Create an Activity

GOAL:

Activity	Materials	Evaluation

TEACHING CHARACTER IN THE MIDDLE GRADES

Create an Activity

GOAL:

Activity	Materials	Evaluation